TALKING ABOUT PARTICULARS

International Library of Philosophy and Scientific Method

EDITOR: TED HONDERICH

A Catalogue of books already published in the
International Library of Philosophy and Scientific Method
will be found at the end of this volume

Talking
About
Particulars

Jack W. Meiland

NEW YORK
HUMANITIES PRESS

*First published
in the United States of America* 1970
*by Humanities Press Inc.
303 Park Avenue South
New York, N.Y.* 10010

© *J. Meiland* 1970

SBN 391 00056 X

111
M513t

72-4804

Printed in Great Britain

CONTENTS

v

To my father and mother

ACKNOWLEDGEMENTS

I have benefited from several discussions with Arthur Burks and C. B. Martin on two topics dealt with in this book. I am also grateful for the helpful comments made by Ted Honderich and by my students in Philosophy 605 and 435 at the University of Michigan during 1967 and 1968 on an earlier draft of this book.

The Rackham Graduate School of the University of Michigan provided funds for typing the final draft of the manuscript. I am indebted to Mrs. Alice Gantt for her care and accuracy in typing the several drafts of this book.

INTRODUCTION

Language is clearly an essential and pervasive part of our lives. Our use of language has often been cited as that which differentiates human beings from the animals—as that which makes us human. It forms the backbone of our culture. Some claim that to learn a quite different language from one's own can result in learning a new way of thinking. Others have claimed that the way in which we think about things is at least influenced by the language that we use. One thing is clear, however: although language has a number of different uses, a very large part of its utility and importance to us stems from our being able to use language to talk about the world. And a large part of being able to talk about the world consists in being able to talk about particular, individual persons and things in the world.

In view of this fact about language, one would hope that philosophers, linguists, and others interested in the relation between language and the world would devote a good deal of attention to our talk about particular individuals. Unfortunately, I think that it is fair to say that this hope has so far been largely unrealized. It has been recognized that speakers talk about particular individuals, and philosophers have often used the term 'refer' to name this activity. They have talked about "the referring use of language" and "referring expressions", and have distinguished between "the theory of meaning" and "the theory of reference". But most of the work done in the philosophy of language up to the present has concentrated on meaning—on the kinds of meaning that an expression can have and on what it is for an expression to have meaning—and on categorizing the various kinds of jobs that can be done by using linguistic expressions. Relatively little has been done on the nature of referring and on the conditions under which speakers perform this activity successfully or unsuccessfully. In view of the importance of referring in talking about the world, this is an unsatisfactory situation.

This book is an attempt to contribute to our understanding of the relation between language and the world. I take referring to be an activity performed by speakers when they employ certain linguistic expressions, particularly names and definite descriptions. I start from a definite and specific problem about referring— what I call "the problem of ambiguous reference". In dealing with this problem, I set forth and argue for general theses about what is involved in referring successfully to a particular individual and, in the last chapter, about what it is for a statement to be about a particular individual. I am especially concerned to establish what I take to be the central role of the speaker's intentions in our talk about particular persons and things.

Author's note
A sentence is a group of words, while a statement is what a person says by uttering a sentence. Throughout this book double quotes generally indicate statements, while single quotes indicate the words (sentences) which can be used in making statements. Thus, the following is a statement about a statement: "John is six feet tall" is false. And the following is a statement about the sentence used in making the statement talked about above: 'John is six feet tall' has five words. Secondly, the expression 'a statement of the form " . . . " ' is to be understood as meaning 'a statement made by using a sentence of the form " . . . " '.

I

THE PROBLEM OF AMBIGUOUS
REFERENCE

Suppose that a speaker makes the statement "John will go to New York next week". Suppose, further, that there is more than one individual having the name 'John'. It is clear that the speaker's statement can be about one and only one of the individuals named 'John' even though the name 'John' *is a name of other individuals as well*. In virtue of what does the speaker succeed in referring to only one of these individuals? What renders the speaker's statement a statement which is about only one, and a certain particular one of these individuals? I will call this "the problem of ambiguous reference". It is this problem and several closely related questions that I will discuss in this book.

The problem of ambiguous reference can be put in a slightly different way. Suppose that someone is asked why this statement is about this particular individual, John, and says "This statement is about John because the speaker used John's name in making the statement". It can then be replied "But the name 'John' is a name of many other individuals too, and yet the statement is not a statement about any of those other individuals". This reply points out that as an instrument of referring the name 'John' is ambiguous. This name is the name of more than one individual and so can be used to refer to a number of different individuals. Therefore, the reason why this statement is about this particular individual cannot be *merely* that the speaker used that individual's name. In this book I will discuss two theories, the Context Theory of Referring and the Abbreviation Theory of Referring, which purport to provide satisfactory solutions to this problem, and I will propose and defend my own theory, the Intention–Description Theory of Referring.

This problem is a problem about "aboutness" and about "referring" themselves and not a problem just about the use of names. In setting forth this problem above, I gave an example which involved the use of the name 'John'. But exactly the same problem can arise in connection with the use of referring expressions other than names. Let us call expressions of the form 'The . . .'—for example, 'The Senator' and 'The person in Room 1215'—"descriptive referring phrases". (Expressions of this form will also be called "descriptive phrases" and "descriptions", the term 'description' thus being used in this book in a way which is quite different from that in which it is ordinarily used.) Then the same problem can be put in the following way. Suppose that a speaker makes the statement "The Senator is in Washington"; the descriptive referring phrase 'The Senator' is one which is satisfied by more than one individual in the sense that there is more than one individual who is a Senator and consequently there is more than one individual about whom this descriptive referring phrase can be used to make a statement; this being the case, what is it that renders the speaker's statement a statement about a particular one of these individuals rather than about another of these individuals? Since this problem is thus a problem in the theory of referring and not just a problem concerning the use of names, theories which purport to provide solutions to this problem must be general theories of referring and not just theories about the use of names.

In addition to the problem set forth above, we will discuss a number of other central issues in the theory of referring, including the following: is there a descriptive element in the use of a name—for example, is it the case that a name is or abbreviates a descriptive phrase? In order to succeed in referring to an individual by using a name, must the speaker use a name which is in fact a name of that individual or can he use a name which is not a name of that individual? What is it for a statement to be about a particular individual rather than about some other individual?

The problem of ambiguous reference is my central concern in this book. Before turning to this problem, however, I must deal with a fundamental objection, namely that statements in which the

2

speaker ostensibly refers to a single particular individual in fact involve no such reference to any individual whatsoever. If this objection were correct, there would be no phenomenon for which a theory of referring could account. In Chapter II I try to show that this objection is not cogent. Chapter II should also help to make clear what sort of referring I am talking about in this book. Having shown that there is such a thing as referring, I turn to the conditions of successful referring and hence to the problem of ambiguous reference. The Context Theory of Referring is described and rejected in Chapter III. It is shown to provide no solution to the problem of ambiguous reference and in fact to be unsatisfactory even in unproblematic cases of referring. A more serious contender, the Abbreviation Theory of Referring, is presented in Chapters IV and V. Since this theory is widely held but little discussed, I spend Chapter IV developing this theory in detail. In Chapters VI and VII I put forward my own theory, the Intention–Description Theory of Referring. I show how it handles ambiguous reference, exhibit the ways in which it is superior to the Abbreviation Theory of Referring, and defend it against a number of objections. When a speaker refers successfully to an individual, he (normally) makes a statement which is about that individual. What it is for a statement to be about an individual is discussed in Chapter VIII.

The problem of ambiguous reference has not often been discussed. There is a quite different problem (or set of problems) connected with reference which have been discussed at great length and which must be sharply distinguished from the problem which I have set forth above. Suppose that someone utters the sentence 'The present king of France is bald' and there is no present king of France; has the speaker said anything true or false; is what the speaker says about anyone? Russell and Strawson have made the most important contributions to the discussion of this problem. I will not be primarily concerned with this problem in this book. Instead, I am primarily concerned with the quite different problem of ambiguous reference. The problem of ambiguous reference arises when there is more than one individual who "fits" the referring expression, while the Russell–Strawson problem arises when there is not even one such individual.

However, although I will not discuss the Russell–Strawson

problem, what I do say about the problem of ambiguous reference depends to some extent on certain doctrines expounded by Strawson. I distinguish between sentences and statements, much as Strawson does. A sentence is the group of words or physical symbols which the speaker employs, while a statement is what the speaker says by uttering sentences. My notion of statement, though, may well be different from that of Strawson. This notion, and the sense of 'said' in which a statement is what the speaker says, will be discussed in detail in Chapter IV and the following chapters where this notion of statement becomes crucial. In particular, I will there explain what I mean by 'same statement'. Second, I will argue, against Russell, that ostensible subject–predicate statements are not existence statements. Third, I will assume that Strawson is generally correct in maintaining that if there is no present king of France, the speaker has said nothing true or false or, as it is sometimes put, made no statement when he utters the words (the sentence) 'The present king of France is bald'. However, I will not argue for this assumption here.[1] There are a number of problems with this Strawsonian position. For example, it is not yet clear precisely what relation the term 'presupposition' denotes. But I believe that some version of Strawson's general view will be found to be satisfactory. On the basis of this assumption, then, I will talk about the speaker's "trying to make a statement" by uttering a certain sentence and "succeeding in making a statement" by uttering a certain sentence. This distinction is closely related to what is said in Section 10 of Chapter VI about two senses of the expressions 'referring to someone' and 'talking about someone'. A speaker is referring to or talking about someone in the first sense of these expressions when he tries to make a statement which is about that individual. The speaker is referring to or talking about someone in the

---

[1] Strawson originally put forward this type of position in 'On Referring', *Mind*, LIX (1950), reprinted in A. Flew (ed.), *Essays in Conceptual Analysis* (Macmillan, London, 1956). This view is also put forward in P. Strawson, *Introduction to Logical Theory* (Methuen, London, 1952), pp. 174–9. It is criticized by Sellars and further defended by Strawson in *The Philosophical Review*, LXIII (1954). Very recent works on this topic which should be consulted include L. Linsky, *Referring* (Routledge & Kegan Paul, London, 1967); Ted Honderich, 'On the Theory of Descriptions', *Proceedings of the Aristotelian Society*, N.S. LXIX (1968–9); G. C. Nerlich, 'Presupposition and Entailment', *American Philosophical Quarterly*, II (1965). Further references will be found in the bibliography of Linsky's *Referring*.

second sense of these expressions when he succeeds in making a statement about that individual (or when he simply makes a statement which *is* about that individual without trying, and hence without succeeding, in doing so). This distinction will be elaborated in Chapter VI, but it would be well for the reader to keep it in mind during earlier chapters too.

Three further points about my terminology must be emphasized. When a speaker uses a name or a description in a referring way, he is trying to say something about (make a statement about) a particular individual. It must be clearly understood what I mean by 'a particular individual' here. I mean, for example, that the speaker is trying to say something about the particular person Arturo Toscanini when he uses the name 'Arturo Toscanini' and not about just any one person of the group of people who may happen to have the name 'Arturo Toscanini'. I mean the same sort of thing when I say that in using the descriptive phrase 'the conductor of the NBC Symphony Orchestra' the speaker is trying to say something about a particular individual and not about just any one of the persons who have conducted that orchestra. We must distinguish among three things here:

    (i) saying something about a *group* of individuals
    (ii) saying something about *any one* individual of a certain class
    (iii) saying something about a *particular*, *specific*, *single* individual.

In this book I will be concerned with the third of these activities. This third activity is what I mean by "referring to an individual".[1]

It should be clear by now that I am using the term 'referring' in such a way that reference is closely connected with aboutness. I use these terms in such a way that when the *speaker* refers to Toscanini, the *statement* which he thereby makes is *about* Toscanini. But there is a problem about aboutness which must be dealt with at the outset. Consider the statement "Jones bought Smith's car". Whom or what is this statement about? I think that we must

---

[1] In using the name 'Arturo Toscanini' to refer to an individual, the speaker is not trying to make a statement about just any individual who has that name. The speaker would not regard his attempt as successful if he had succeeded in making a statement about *some one* person who has or had this name. We will, however, see in Section 14 of Chapter VI that ultimately the speaker can be viewed as trying to make a statement about just any individual of a certain class provided that that class has only one member.

distinguish here between *mention* and other types of aboutness. A good case can be made for saying that Jones, Smith, and the car are mentioned by the speaker when he makes this statement, particularly if the statement is put as "Jones bought the car of Smith". But it also seems to me that there can be situations in which we would want to say that this statement was about Jones rather than Smith or the car, or alternatively, more about Jones than about Smith or the car. For example, the speaker and hearer might have been talking exclusively about Jones up to now, and this statement might have been an answer to the question "Has Jones bought a car yet?" The term 'about' is used in this way, the way in which this statement is about Jones rather than Smith or the car. It is also used in a second way, a way such that this statement is about all three equally—Jones, Smith, and the car. I will use the term 'about' in this latter sense—in the sense in which this statement is equally about Jones, Smith, and the car. That is, I am using the term 'about' in the sense of 'mention'. It seems to me likely that this second sense of 'about' is more fundamental than and underlies the first sense in that a necessary condition of a statement's being about someone in the first sense of 'about' is that the statement be about that person in the second sense of 'about', that is, that that person be mentioned in the statement.

Finally, there is a great difference between what I call "referring to an individual" and what I call "referring the hearer to an individual". (This distinction is discussed further in Section 11 of Chapter VI.) The former consists in making a statement which is about that individual. The latter consists in getting the hearer to identify correctly the individual about whom one is making, or trying to make, a statement or about whom one is trying to convey information even without making a statement about that individual. It is the former activity—referring to an individual—and its associated problem of ambiguous reference that constitutes the main topic of this book.

II

DOES REFERRING TAKE PLACE?

1 *Introduction*

Before proceeding to discuss particular theories of referring, we must consider an objection which is an objection to all theories of referring. It is this: there is no activity for which a theory of referring can account; for in fact speakers never refer to individuals in the sense of making statements which are about particular individuals, nor can speakers do so. In the next sections, I will present and discuss an argument supporting this objection. Then I will consider a more restricted position of this type which has been put forward. This discussion should also make clearer what I mean by "referring to a particular individual".

2 *Are all ostensible subject–predicate statements in fact existence statements?*

The argument supporting the above objection that I wish to discuss is this. It is first claimed that every statement which is made by using a sentence of grammatical subject–predicate form having a name or a descriptive phrase as its grammatical subject is in fact an existence statement. That is, such statements are identical with statements which can be made by using sentences of the form 'There exists . . . '. This type of claim has been made by Russell among others.[1] Russell's view on ostensible subject–predicate statements gives rise to the objection to be discussed in this chapter. We will discuss two types of existence statements: those made by using sentences of the form 'There exists one and

[1] B. Russell, *Introduction to Mathematical Philosophy* (George Allen & Unwin, London, 1919), pp. 167–80.

7

only one . . . ' and those made by using sentences of the form
'There exists at least one . . . '. Thus, on this view, the statement
"The man in Room 1512 of the Empire State Building is a
sociologist" is said to be identical with (on one version of this
position) the statement "There exists one and only one individual
who is a man in Room 1512 of the Empire State Building and
is a sociologist" or (on another version of this theory) with
the statement "There exists at least one man in Room 1512 of the
Empire State Building who is a sociologist".

Thus, the first step in the argument which I am presenting is
this: all subject–predicate statements of the type in question are
existence statements. The next step in the argument is this: no
existence statement is about an individual. If such statements are
about anything, they are about "the world" and assert that the
world contains an individual (or one and only one individual)
having certain properties. Since every ostensible subject–predicate
statement is identical with some existence statement, and no
existence statement is about a particular individual, no ostensible
subject–predicate statement is about a particular individual. But
I will use the expression 'succeeding in referring' in such a way
that a speaker *succeeds in referring* to a particular individual only if
he makes a statement (or asks a question, and so on) which is
about that particular individual. Since no ostensible subject-
predicate is or can be about an individual, it is not possible for a
speaker to succeed in referring to an individual by making such
a statement (although a speaker can, perhaps, nevertheless try to
refer to an individual by making such a statement). Theories of
referring—such as the Intention–Description Theory of Referring
and the Abbreviation Theory of Referring—purport to give the
conditions under which the speaker succeeds in referring to a particular individual by making such a statement. Since a speaker
cannot succeed in doing so, there are no such conditions and there
is no such phenomenon for which such a theory can account.

This argument would be shown to be unsound if it were shown
that ostensible subject–predicate statements involving names or
descriptions—that is, statements made by using sentences having
a subject–predicate grammatical form where the grammatical
subject is a name or a description—are not identical with existential statements. Alternatively, this argument would be shown to

8

be unsound if it were shown that at least some existential statements are or can be about particular individuals. I will adopt the first alternative. I will attempt to show that ostensible subject–predicate statements are not identical with existential statements. And I will do this by showing that there can be situations in which an ostensible subject–predicate statement has a different truth-value from that of the putatively corresponding existential statement.

Let us first consider the version of this theory which claims that the ostensible subject–predicate statement "The man in Room 1512 of the Empire State Building is a sociologist" is identical with the statement "There is one and only one man in Room 1512 of the Empire State Building who is a sociologist". Suppose that there are two people who are men, who are in Room 1512 of the Empire State Building, and who are sociologists. In this situation the statement "There is one and only one individual who is a man in Room 1512 of the Empire State Building and who is a sociologist" is false. But it is simply a fact that what the speaker says when he says "The man in Room 1512 of the Empire State Building is a sociologist" might very well be true. This is a fact about our actual use of language. It is a fact from which a theory of language must start or, at least, of which it must take account. This fact—that what the speaker says might very well be true—shows that the speaker who utters the sentence 'The man in Room 1512 of the Empire State Building is a sociologist' is not thereby making an existential statement of the type in question. It shows that there is a difference between the two types of statements in question. This difference is then accounted for by saying that the existential statement is *not* about any of the individuals having the mentioned properties while the ostensible subject–predicate statement *may* very well be about just one of these individuals. The two statements in question are about different things. The existential statement is about, if anything, the world; it says something about the world. But the subject–predicate statement may well be about just one individual and his properties independently of the properties of other individuals in the world. It must be emphasized that what I have said so far is independent of any particular theory of referring. I have so far merely relied on a fact of which all such theories must take cognizance.

9

DOES REFERRING TAKE PLACE?

It might now be suggested that since the existential statement "There is at least one individual who is a man in Room 1512 of the Empire State Building and is a sociologist" is not false in the situation described above, it is *this* existential statement which should be taken as identical with the subject–predicate statement in question. This subject–predicate statement will then not be about any particular individual. Of course, this assumes that such existential statements are not about particular individuals, an assumption which can be supported in the following way. Let us again suppose that there are two individuals who are men, who are in Room 1512 of the Empire State Building, and who are sociologists. In this situation, the statement "There exists at least one man who is in Room 1512 of the Empire State Building and who is a sociologist" cannot be said to be about either of these individuals. There is no reason to say that this statement is about one of these individuals rather than the other. Consequently, if an ostensible subject–predicate statement were identical with such a statement, then if there were two or more such individuals, the ostensible subject–predicate statement could not be said to be about a particular individual.

However, the ostensible subject–predicate statement "The man in Room 1512 of the Empire State Building is a sociologist" is not identical with the statement "There exists at least one individual who is a man, who is in Room 1512 of the Empire State Building, and who is a sociologist". Let us suppose that there are two men who are in Room 1512 of the Empire State Building but that only one of them is a sociologist. In this situation the existential state-ment is true. For there is a man in that room who is a sociologist. But it is a fact that the ostensible subject–predicate statement may very well be false (although it could be true too). That the latter could be false while the existential statement is true shows that these two statements are not identical with one another.

It might be objected that so far I have shown only that the ostensible subject–predicate statement is not identical with an existential statement in cases where two or more individuals satisfy the description 'The man in Room 1512 . . . '. It is still possible that in other sorts of cases the former could be identical with an existential statement—for example, in cases in which only one individual satisfies this description. What the objector says here implies that what statement a speaker makes depends in at least some cases on the state of the world and in particular on how many individuals satisfy a certain description. On the objector's view, if more than one individual satisfies the uttered description, then the speaker makes a non-existential statement, while if only one individual does so, the speaker makes an existential statement. However, it seems that what statement, or at least what type of statement, a speaker makes does not depend on the state of the world; instead it is both the fact that he makes a statement at all and the truth-value of what he says that depend on the state of the world. But let us assume that it is possible for the type of statement which the speaker makes to depend on the state of the world. And let us assume that when only one individual satisfies the uttered description, the ostensible subject–predicate statement is identical with an existential statement. With which type of existential statement is it identical? Is the ostensible statement made by uttering a sentence of the form 'There exists one and only one . . . '? Or is it identical with one made by uttering a sentence of the form 'There exists at least one . . . '? In a situation in which there is one and only one individual who satisfies the uttered description, these two existential statements will have the same truth-value. Consequently, there is no reason to say that the ostensible subject–predicate statement is identical with one of them rather than with the other. Hence, it must be said that this statement is identical with neither of these statements in this sort of case.

3 Aboutness and 'knowing who the individual is'

Now I wish to consider a more restricted theory of the type just discussed. This theory does not maintain, as did the previous one, that referring never takes place. But it does maintain that referring takes place only in a very limited number of cases, namely only when the speaker is in the presence of the individual to whom he is trying to refer. Only then can a speaker's statement be about a particular individual. This theory has been put forward by Prior. If Prior is right, referring takes place relatively rarely and is a fairly unimportant activity. My aim, then, in discussing Prior's view is to show that referring is an activity which it is important that we understand because of its pervasiveness in our linguistic behaviour.

Prior seems to believe that in at least many of those cases in which a speaker appears to be referring to and talking about an individual, the speaker is in fact not doing so. What the speaker is doing in these cases is making an existential statement. For example, Prior claims that when a speaker says now (as opposed to saying in, say, 46 B.C.) "Julius Caesar crossed the Rubicon",

> ... it would be quite misleading to say that ... [this statement] is only about the *name* 'Julius Caesar', or even that it is about that name at all; it isn't strictly speaking 'about' anyone or anything, i.e. there is no one of whom I say that he crossed the Rubicon; but I do say *that someone* crossed the Rubicon, and I have previously said (among much else) that this same someone was called 'Julius Caesar'.[1]

Prior thus seems to hold that when a speaker now utters the sentence 'Julius Caesar crossed the Rubicon', he thereby makes a statement identical with that which he would make if he had used a sentence such as 'Someone who lived in Rome, who was called "Julius Caesar", and who conquered Gaul, crossed the Rubicon'. Since statements made by uttering sentences of the form 'Someone who ... ' are identical with statements made by uttering sentences of the form 'There exists ... ', on Prior's view the speaker makes an existential statement when he says "Julius Caesar crossed the Rubicon".[2]

But if the term 'Julius Caesar' does not have a referring function in this case—if the speaker does not use this term to render his statement a statement *about* a particular individual—then what is the function of this term in this case? Prior says that in this case the term 'Julius Caesar' has the function of "cross-reference" rather than that of reference.[3] Apparently, what he means here is that the speaker who uses the name 'Julius Caesar' is not referring

---

[1] A. Prior, 'Oratio Obliqua', *Aristotelian Society Supplementary Volume*, XXXVIII (1963), p. 125.

[2] That Prior believes that statements made by using sentences of the form 'Someone who ... ' are such existence statements is shown by what he says at the bottom of p. 126 of 'Oratio Obliqua', where he speaks of " ... the *other* sort of case, in which there is no object to which we stand in the relation of believing that *it* is or does such-and-such, but we merely *believe that there is* an object that is or does the thing in question". Since, as we shall see, Prior holds that what is true of believing in this sort of case is also true of referring, this shows that he believes that the speaker who now says "Julius Caesar crossed the Rubicon" is making an existential statement.

[3] *Ibid.*, pp. 124-5.

to the individual (except when the speaker is in the presence of that individual)[1] but is referring back to statements previously made by one or another speaker or to beliefs held by the speaker or someone else or to both such statements and such beliefs. The speaker is referring back to statements which have been made by using the name 'Julius Caesar' or to beliefs which would be expressed by using that name or to both. Thus, when a speaker utters a sentence in such a case by using a sentence of the form 'Julius Caesar crossed the Rubicon', he makes a statement which can also be made by uttering a sentence of the form 'Someone who is named "Julius Caesar" and is $\emptyset$ and U is also Θ', where $\emptyset$ and U are properties mentioned in previous statements or in the expression of certain beliefs (and Θ is the predicate property of the statement, namely "having crossed the Rubicon"). Apparently Prior believes that given any use of the name 'Julius Caesar' about an individual who is not in the presence of the speaker, there will be a context in which that use occurs and which specifies what beliefs and previous statements are being cross-referred (or referred back) to. Then $\emptyset$ and U are those properties mentioned in the specified beliefs and previous statements. In a case in which the context does not specify any such beliefs or previous statements, Prior would apparently say that the statement "Julius Caesar crossed the Rubicon" is identical with the statement "Someone named 'Julius Caesar' crossed the Rubicon". That is, in such a case the speaker's statement would be identical with a statement made by using a sentence of the form 'Someone who is $\emptyset$ is Θ' where $\emptyset$ stands for the property "being named 'Julius Caesar'", that is, where the only property mentioned, in addition to the predicate property "having crossed the Rubicon", is the property of being named 'Julius Caesar'. For in this case no previous statements or beliefs mentioning other properties are being cross-referred to.

Exactly what is it that the speaker can make cross-reference to? First, it does not seem that the speaker can be making cross-reference to beliefs of *both* the speaker and the hearer. Suppose that the hearer believes that someone named 'Julius Caesar' invaded Russia. The speaker could nevertheless truly deny that in using the name 'Julius Caesar' in the presence of such a hearer, he

[1] *Ibid.*, p. 125.

was making a statement of the type "Someone who was named 'Julius Caesar' and who invaded Russia . . . ". A speaker does not necessarily make a statement involving a certain property just because a hearer believes that someone having a certain name has that property. After all, there could be two hearers one of whom had a belief expressed by a statement of the type "Someone who was named 'Julius Caesar' and who invaded Russia . . . " and the other of whom had a belief expressed by a statement of the type "Someone who was named 'Julius Caesar' and who never invaded Russia . . . ". And if the speaker did cross-refer to the beliefs of his hearers, the speaker would be making a statement of the type "Someone who was named 'Julius Caesar' and who invaded Russia and who never invaded Russia . . . ", which the speaker is, of course, in fact not doing at all. This also shows that the speaker is not cross-referring to the hearer's beliefs even when he knows that his hearers have these beliefs.

So it seems that if the speaker cross-refers to beliefs at all, he cross-refers only to his own beliefs. But to which of his own beliefs is the speaker cross-referring here? The set of beliefs to which the speaker is cross-referring cannot be described by Prior as the set of the speaker's own beliefs which are about Julius Caesar, for, as we shall see, Prior believes that *none* of the speaker's beliefs can now be *about* the individual Julius Caesar. This set must instead be described by Prior as the set of the speaker's beliefs whose expression would or can involve the use of the name 'Julius Caesar'. Let us suppose that the speaker does have such beliefs and says "Julius Caesar crossed the Rubicon". According to Prior, the speaker is thereby saying "Someone who was named 'Julius Caesar', who had $\emptyset$, and who had U, crossed the Rubicon", where $\emptyset$ and U are representative of properties some of which would be mentioned in expressions of beliefs of the speaker belonging to the set of beliefs specified above. Now let us suppose that in fact this speaker believes truly that there existed only two individuals named 'Julius Caesar', both of whom crossed the Rubicon, one and only one of whom had $\emptyset$, and the other of whom (and only he) had U. The speaker says "Julius Caesar crossed the Rubicon". Which of the following statements has the speaker made: (*a*) "Someone who was named 'Julius Caesar' and was $\emptyset$ crossed the Rubicon"; (*b*) "Someone who was named

'Julius Caesar' and was U crossed the Rubicon"; (c) "Someone who was named 'Julius Caesar' and was $\emptyset$ and U crossed the Rubicon"?

The speaker was not necessarily making statement (c) in this situation; for in this situation statement (c) is false while the statement "Julius Caesar crossed the Rubicon" can be true. And although, both (a) and (b) are true statements in this situation, there is no way of determining on the basis of Prior's theory which of these two statements the speaker made. For example, we cannot say that the speaker made statement (a) because he was referring to the individual named 'Julius Caesar' who had $\emptyset$. For, on Prior's view, the speaker is not referring to any individual at all in making this statement. Yet a speaker can certainly make a determinate statement in this situation. It seems that in view of this possible case, the speaker should be taken as cross-referring only to statements made previously in that context by use of the name 'Julius Caesar' and not to beliefs of either the hearer or himself.

But to which statements made by using the name 'Julius Caesar' is the speaker cross-referring? Is he, for example, cross-referring to all such previous statements in that context? Let us suppose that the statement "Julius Caesar invaded Russia" had been previously made in that context. Certainly if the speaker believed that this statement was false, he would not cross-refer to it when he made his own statement "Julius Caesar crossed the Rubicon". For the speaker would not himself make the statement "Someone who was named 'Julius Caesar' and who invaded Russia crossed the Rubicon". Does the speaker then cross-refer to all and only previous such statements which he believes to be true? Let us suppose that the speaker believes the previously made statement "Julius Caesar invaded Russia" to be true and hence that in making his own statement, the speaker cross-refers to this statement. That is, in making his own statement, the speaker makes the statement "Someone who was named 'Julius Caesar' and who invaded Russia crossed the Rubicon". But then he makes a false statement. And yet a speaker can say "Julius Caesar crossed the Rubicon" and thereby make a true statement even if the speaker falsely believes that Julius Caesar also invaded Russia. This seems to show that the speaker does not even cross-refer to every previous such statement which he believes to be true.

One can reply to this objection by using a device to be discussed in later chapters. This device is the expression 'an individual who has a sufficient number of . . . ' where the dots stand for properties. An individual can satisfy such a description without having every one of the mentioned properties. Similarly, Prior can say that a speaker can make a true statement by cross-referring to a group of statements some of which are false in the way indicated above because the speaker's statement is of the type 'Someone who was named "Julius Caesar" and has a sufficient number of . . . crossed the Rubicon'. The dots here stand for properties mentioned in statements previously made in that context by using the name 'Julius Caesar'. And such a statement can be true even if no one individual has or had all of the properties mentioned in statements previously made in that context by using the name 'Julius Caesar'. So it appears that what Prior should say here is this: the speaker cross-refers to all such statements previously made in that context which he believes to be true; and the speaker's own statement is of the type 'Someone who was named "Julius Caesar" and had a sufficient number of . . . crossed the Rubicon'.

Prior discusses only names but it is clear that he would have to say that descriptions can be used in only a cross-referring way in certain cases too. For the reasons given for the position that names are used in many cases to cross-refer rather than to refer—which reasons we will examine in a moment—are reasons supporting the position that in these cases the speaker cannot in *any* way make a statement which is about a particular individual by uttering the sentence in question. So Prior cannot allow descriptions to be used to make statements which are about these individuals, since he seems to claim that in these cases no statements by the speaker will be about these individuals. Hence he must say that descriptions are used to cross-refer rather than to refer in these cases.

It might be objected at this point that if Prior does say that in these cases descriptions are used to cross-refer rather than to refer, then he cannot show that the statements "The individual who is Ø is U" and "The individual who is U is Ø" are two different statements. For on his view the speakers who make these statements while not in the presence of whoever has the properties in question make existential statements. And since the order in which properties are mentioned in an existential statement does not affect which statement is being made, both of these speakers are making the statement "There exists an individual who is Ø and 𝒰". So on Prior's view these two speakers are making the same statement. But in fact these two speakers are not making the same statement. However, this objection is not sound. Prior's view can show that these two speakers are making different statements. For each statement, while not containing a different *referring* expression, does contain a different *cross-referring* expression. The expression 'the individual who is Ø' can be used to cross-refer to some statements—for instance, the statement "The individual who is Ø is also Θ"—to which the expression 'the individual who is 𝒰' cannot be used to cross-refer. For the former expression can be used to cross-refer only to statements in which the property Ø is mentioned, while the latter expression can be used to cross-refer only to statements in which the property 𝒰 is mentioned. And cross-reference to different statements results in the *speakers'* statements being different. If a speaker cross-refers to one set of statements which mention certain properties, his own statement will mention those properties, while if he cross-refers to another set of statements which mention other properties, his own statement will mention those other properties instead. Thus, two speakers who use these two descriptions ('the individual who is Ø' and 'the individual who is 𝒰') may well cross-refer to different sets of statements and hence each may make a different statement from that made by the other.

What is Prior's argument for his claim that certain expressions are used to cross-refer rather than to refer in certain cases? His argument concerns beliefs. But if his argument concerning beliefs is sound, it can be used—as Prior does use it—to support his position on referring. This is so for the following two reasons. His argument is intended to show that certain beliefs which are allegedly about particular individuals are in fact not about those individuals. First, the same arguments can be given to show that certain statements which are allegedly about particular individuals are in fact not about those individuals, if both beliefs and statements are about particular individuals in the same sense of 'about'. Secondly, there is a certain relation between certain beliefs and certain statements, namely that those statements can be used to express those beliefs. If Prior can show that certain beliefs which seem to be about particular individuals—such as the belief that Julius Caesar crossed the Rubicon—are in fact not about those particular individuals, he will have shown that the statements which express those beliefs and which also seem to be about those particular individuals are in fact not about those particular individuals.

Prior's argument for his position is this. He first claims that a necessary condition of a person's having a belief which is about a particular individual is that that person "know who that individual is".[1] At another point Prior puts this same requirement by saying that it is necessary that the person be able to "identify" that individual.[2] Prior would hold that a person who did not know who Charles de Gaulle is or who could not correctly identify Charles de Gaulle could not have a belief that is about Charles de Gaulle. One of the situations—and apparently the only situation—in which a person can have a belief which is about a certain individual, according to Prior, is that in which the person is observing that individual. Prior does say that this is a sufficient condition of a person's having a belief which is about that individual when the expression of that belief would apparently be a statement in making which the speaker is talking about that individual. It is not clear, however, which beliefs of the observer would be about the observed individual, on Prior's view. For example, let us suppose that the person is observing Harold Wilson and believes falsely that he is observing Charles de Gaulle. The person believes that Charles de Gaulle was elected in 1964. Is his belief that Charles de Gaulle was elected in 1964 a belief about the individual whom he is observing, even though that individual is not Charles de Gaulle? It is not clear how we should answer this question.

Prior then says that a person's present belief that Julius Caesar crossed the Rubicon—and hence the statement "Julius Caesar crossed the Rubicon" which expresses this belief—are not about Julius Caesar because the person does not know who Julius Caesar is.[3] Presumably, moreover, Prior would have to say that the person not only does not know who Julius Caesar is but cannot come to know who Julius Caesar is. One argument which Prior could give for this claim is this: the only way in which he

<hr />

[1] *Op. cit.*, p. 122.   [2] *Ibid.*, p. 123.   [3] *Ibid.*, p. 124.

could come to know this is by hearing statements which are about Julius Caesar; but all such statements will, for the same reason, involve cross-reference rather than reference and so will not themselves be about Julius Caesar. Hence he will not learn facts about Julius Caesar nor, therefore, learn who Julius Caesar is. Prior does not explain what he means by the expressions 'knowing who that individual is' and 'being able to identify that individual'. He does say two things about this. First, he says that it is not sufficient for knowing who U Thant is that the person know that he is the individual referred to by someone else as "U Thant".[1] Second, he says that when the individual is "in sight" or is being observed, then the person knows who that individual is.[2] Furthermore, he seems to imply that when the individual is "out of sight", the person does not know who the individual is.[3] That is, Prior seems to hold that the individual's "being in sight" is both a necessary condition and a sufficient condition of the person's knowing who that individual is and of being able to identify that individual. If this is Prior's position, then he is not using the expressions 'knowing who the individual is' and 'being able to identify that individual' in their usual senses. For in their usual senses, a person can know who an individual is and is able to identify that individual if the person knows some properties which, taken together, are properties only of that individual. Thus, in the usual sense of 'knowing who an individual is', a person can know who an individual is without being in the presence of that individual. A person can truly say "I know who U Thant is; he is the current Secretary-General of the United Nations".

What is Prior's argument for his claim that a necessary condition of a person's belief being about an individual is that the person knows who the individual is in Prior's sense of this latter expression? Prior says that unless his position is adopted, one must say that a person believes that, for example, zotz is glotz if the person believes that the alleged statement "Zotz is glotz" is true.[4] Apparently what Prior means here is that if one says that a person can believe that Julius Caesar crossed the Rubicon and thus have a belief which is about Julius Caesar without knowing who Julius Caesar is (in Prior's sense of that expression), then one must say that a person can have beliefs about zotz even if that person

---

[1] *Ibid.*, p. 124.   [2] *Ibid.*, pp. 123, 125.   [3] *Ibid.*, p. 125.   [4] *Ibid.*, p. 124.

does not know who or what zotz is—in fact, even though there is no such thing as zotz. But this is not correct. One does not have to adopt Prior's very strong sense of the expression 'knowing who the individual is' in order not to have to say that a person believes that zotz is glotz just because he believes that what someone says when he says "Zotz is glotz" is true. One need only adopt the ordinary sense of 'knowing who the individual is' for this. We can require that in order for a person to believe that zotz is glotz, that person must know who or what zotz is, in the sense of being able to give a set of properties which together belong only to zotz or of being able to recognize zotz when in its presence. Then it is not sufficient for a person to believe that zotz is glotz, that he believes that what someone says when he utters the sentence 'Zotz is glotz' is true. For since there is no such thing as zotz, the person cannot give such a set of properties or recognize zotz, and hence on our view cannot be said to believe that zotz is glotz. But if we do adopt the ordinary sense of the expression 'knowing who the individual is', then it is nevertheless possible for someone to know who Julius Caesar is without being in the presence of Julius Caesar, as shown earlier. Thus, Prior has not shown that no statement made now by using the name 'Julius Caesar' is about Julius Caesar.

In the sense of the expression 'knowing who the individual is' which I have called the ordinary sense, a speaker can know who an individual is even when that individual is not in the presence of the speaker. Hence, the speaker can refer to past individuals, such as Julius Caesar, in so far as knowing who they are is concerned.

Moreover, the speaker can refer to future individuals for the same reason. The speaker can make a statement—for example, "John Smith, the 43rd President of the United States, will be this country's best president in over a century"—which is now about a future individual, in so far as knowing who that individual is is concerned. The speaker can give a set of individuating properties and can thus identify who it is that he is talking about. It might be objected that past individuals exist "in the past" and that is why past individuals can now stand in the relation of now being referred to by some speaker, while future individuals do not exist and hence cannot now stand in any such relation. But surely future individuals can now exist just as much in the future as a past individual now does in the past. It may also be objected that the speaker does not now know, for example, that the 43rd President will be named 'John Smith', and in general that the speaker cannot know that there will be one and only one future individual having the properties which he believes the individual to which he is ostensibly referring to have. But one cannot know, in the case of past individuals, that there is only one such past individual either, as the possibility of a duplicate universe described by Burks shows (see Section 9 of Chapter V)—nor even in the case of present individuals for the same reason. And in any case what is required for successful reference is not that the speaker know that there is one and only one individual satisfying a certain description or having a certain name, but instead that there *be* one and only one such individual. It is certainly possible that there be one and only one such future individual. Hence it is possible to make statements now which are about future particular individuals.

A second objection to Prior's position is this. It was said earlier that the name 'Julius Caesar' can be used to cross-refer to several previous statements one of which is false, and that nevertheless that name can thereby be used to make a true statement. It was said that this could be so because the statement which the speaker makes is of the type "There exists an individual who has a sufficient number of . . . ". However, there could be a situation in which not just one but every statement previously made in that situation by using the name 'Julius Caesar' is false. Then if the speaker uses the name 'Julius Caesar' to cross-refer to these statements, he makes a statement which is false even if it is of the type "There exists an individual who has a sufficient number of $\emptyset$, U, . . . and who is also Θ" (where one of $\emptyset$, U, . . . is the property of being named 'Julius Caesar' and where the rest of $\emptyset$, U, . . . are the properties mentioned in the statements which are cross-referred to). For in a case in which all of the statements cross-referred to are false, it is possible for there to be no individual who has a sufficient number of $\emptyset$, U, . . . And if there is in fact no such individual, then the existential statement is false. But nevertheless, even in such a situation it is possible for a speaker to make a true statement by saying "Julius Caesar crossed the Rubicon". This shows that the name 'Julius Caesar' is not being used to cross-refer to the previous statements in this situation. But then in what way is it being used? It seems that Prior could only say that the name is being used to make the statement "There was an individual named 'Julius Caesar' who crossed the Rubicon", that is, that the name was not being used to cross-refer or to refer but instead to make this type of existential statement. Prior would have to say that the speaker can determine how the name is used— that is, in any situation the speaker can use the name to cross-refer to previous statements or he can refrain from doing so. And when the speaker refrains from doing so, he makes a statement of the type "There exists (or existed) an individual who was named '. . .' and who has (or had) the property $\emptyset$". It is true that the statement "There existed an individual named 'Julius Caesar' who crossed the Rubicon" would be true in the situation which I have described. But now let us suppose that there was only one individual named 'Julius Caesar' and that the speaker uses the name 'Julius Caesar' to cross-refer to a set of previous statements all of which are false but all of which he believes to be true. On Prior's theory, the speaker would have made a false statement, as shown above. But, as I will argue in a later chapter, the speaker—if he had said, for example, "Julius Caesar crossed the Rubicon"— would in fact have made a true statement, since only one individual bore the name 'Julius Caesar'. Consequently, the speaker *could not* have been cross-referring to the previous statements. But Prior must say that the speaker *could* have cross-referred to those statements, for the reasons given above. Hence, Prior's theory is unsatisfactory.

A third objection to Prior's position is this. Let us suppose that there are at least two individuals named 'George Jones'. One of these individuals owns a grocery store while the other is an executive in an aircraft company. Let us also suppose that the speaker says "George Jones is an executive in an aircraft company". The speaker then finds out that the individual named 'George Jones', who lives in Passaic, New Jersey, owns a grocery store. It is possible that the speaker, upon learning this, then will justifiably regard what he said as false. And it is further possible that the speaker will not change his mind about this and will not henceforth regard what he said as true upon learning that there is an individual named 'George Jones' in Cheyenne, Wyoming, who is an executive in an aircraft company. The speaker can still truly say that what he said was false. We would explain this fact by saying that the speaker was referring to one of these individuals rather than another and that his statement was about one of these individuals rather than the other. But on Prior's theory, the speaker's statement is not false in this situation since it is an existential statement. Consequently, Prior's theory is unsatisfactory.

A fourth objection to Prior's view is this. If a speaker makes the statement "Julius Caesar crossed the Rubicon", it is always possible for a hearer to ask the speaker "Which Julius Caesar are you talking about?" How can Prior construe this question on his theory? It seems that he can construe this question only in the following way. Let us suppose that the speaker made his statement in a context in which the name 'Julius Caesar' had not previously been used. Then, on Prior's theory the speaker made the statement "There existed an individual named 'Julius Caesar' who crossed the Rubicon". It seems, then, that the only thing that the hearer can mean, on Prior's theory, when he asks the question "Which Julius Caesar do you mean?" is "Which existence statement would you have made if you had been asked to make a more complete statement (in the sense of specifying more of the individual's properties) than the one which you did make?" For example, suppose that in reply to the hearer's question "Which Julius Caesar did you mean?", the speaker says "The Julius Caesar who lived in Rome in 45 B.C." It seems that on Prior's view this answer would have to be construed as the speaker's saying that he would have made the more complete statement "There existed an individual who was named 'Julius Caesar', who lived in Rome in 45 B.C., and who crossed the Rubicon". That is, it seems that Prior would have to construe the speaker's reply as completing or making more complete the existence statement which the speaker already made or, perhaps, as making this more complete statement itself. But now let us suppose that after the speaker has given the above reply, the hearer asks "Which Julius Caesar who lived in Rome in 45 B.C. do you mean?" And let us suppose that the speaker does not know anything further about which Julius Caesar he meant. The speaker would then say "I don't know which one I was talking about". How can Prior construe *this* statement? There seems to me to be no satisfactory way in which Prior can construe this on his theory. For if the speaker did say this, he would be saying that he had not in fact made any statement at all, that is, had not said anything that is true or false. He would admit that what he said was neither true nor false.[1] But on Prior's theory, what he said would be either true or false since he made an existence statement on that theory. Since, on Prior's view, the speaker has said something true or false in this case, Prior's view is unsatisfactory.

Since Prior's view is unsatisfactory for these reasons, it seems that statements made by using names or descriptive referring phrases which are usually considered to be about, or possibly about, particular individuals are in fact about, or possibly about, particular individuals. Consequently, there is an important and pervasive activity called "referring" for which a theory of referring can account.

[1] It must be noted that, in view of what will be said in Chapter VII, the speaker could have replied "I mean the one who crossed the Rubicon". Then he would have said something true if only one of these individuals had crossed the Rubicon. But if both of them had crossed the Rubicon, he would not have made a statement.

III

THE CONTEXT THEORY OF
REFERRING

---

1 *Statement of this theory*

Now let us return to the main topic of this book—the problem of ambiguous reference.

When one asks people what it is that makes the statement "Fred is the best man for the job" a statement about Fred Jones rather than about Fred Smith, the context is often given full credit for performing this function. It is not easy, though, to find this view expressed in print, partly because philosophers who mention context as important in "securing unique reference" often do not distinguish between rendering a statement one which is about a certain individual on the one hand and making the hearer aware that this statement is about this individual on the other. So one often does not know whether these philosophers are saying that context is important for the former, for the latter, or for both functions. In any case, however, my inquiries have shown that the Context Theory of Referring is widely held as a naïve first approach to the problem of ambiguous reference. Hence this theory is worth some consideration in order to clear the air for a discussion of more serious contenders.

Much hangs, of course, on what is included in "the context". To render this theory distinct from the two theories discussed in later chapters, I will exclude from "the context" (*a*) the speaker's use of a referring expression as an abbreviation and (*b*) the speaker's intentions. A multitude of factors remain, though, as parts of the context, including the occasion of making the statement, who makes the statement and who the hearers are, what they have been talking about earlier, and so on. As an example, let us suppose that a certain Senator's press secretary is talking with some newspaper reporters. The press secretary begins the news conference by making the statement "The Senator plans to go to Europe next month to investigate the prospects for further reciprocal tariff reductions". The press secretary made this statement by using the expression 'The Senator'. This descriptive phrase can be used to refer to many different individuals, since many different individuals are senators. On the Context Theory of Referring, what renders the press secretary's statement a statement about his employer rather than about one of the other senators is, for example, the fact that this particular senator is his employer and that, further, the situation in which the statement is made is a press conference called by the press secretary in his official capacity. On this theory, not only are the reporters justified by this context in taking the press secretary's statement to be about his employer, but also, because of this context, the press secretary's statement *is* about his employer.

Here is another example. Two men are trying to decide which person to nominate for a certain political post. These two men know that there are several people who have expressed interest in the post, only one of whom has the name 'Jones'. One man says to the other: "Jones is the best person for this post". On the Context Theory of Referring, this statement is about the Jones who expressed interest in the post and not about one of the many other individuals named 'Jones' just because this statement was made in the context of their knowing about this individual's having expressed interest in the post (and, perhaps, that each man knows that the other knows this).

It should be noticed that in each of these examples, the context in question contained either something non-linguistic—as in the case of the Senator being the press secretary's employer—or else statements which were not necessarily about the individual whom the statement in question was about—as in the case of Jones expressing interest in the post. The Context Theory of Referring might hold that ultimately the context which determines which individual a statement is about is not wholly set by or does not wholly consist of other statements about that individual. For otherwise it could then be asked what rendered these statements

statements about that particular individual. And if the answer were again "Yet other statements about that individual", a vicious infinite regress would develop. Or else this theory might hold that there are or can be some statements which are about a particular individual not in virtue of the context in which they are made but instead in virtue of some property of these statements alone which they have regardless of the context in which these statements are made. For then the context could be set by or constituted by such "self-determining" statements without the development of such a regress. A third possibility is this: the theory might hold that a context can be set by a group of statements none of which are about any individual. This too would prevent such a regress.

Presumably what the Context Theory of Referring claims is that the used referring expression (the referring expression which the speaker uses to make the statement—for example, 'Jones' or 'The Senator') together with the context pick out one particular individual which the speaker's statement is then about. This theory would hold that it is necessary and sufficient for a statement to be about a particular individual that that individual be "picked out" or indicated by the context together with the used referring expression.

2 *The meaning of 'indicating' or 'picking out'*

But what is meant by saying that the used expression and the context together "pick out" an individual? Does this mean, for example, that given knowledge that a certain referring expression was used by the speaker, and given knowledge about the context, a hearer would come to believe that the individual in question is the individual about whom the speaker is talking? This does not seem to be correct. For given a particular context and a particular used referring expression, a hearer might pick out almost any individual as the one being talked about. Moreover, there might be more than one hearer in a given situation, each of whom identified a different individual as the one being talked about; but the statement is at most about only one of these individuals.

3 *Context indication as a necessary condition of aboutness*

Regardless of exactly what 'indicate' might mean here, it is not the case that indication of an individual by context is a necessary condition of a statement's being about an individual. For the context might be such as to "indicate" more than one individual, even when taken together with the used referring expression. For example, suppose that two people named 'Jones' have expressed interest in the political post and that the speaker had again said "Jones is the best person for this post". The context does not now indicate which of these individuals the statement is about, and yet the statement can easily *be* about one of these individuals rather than the other. It is true that the hearer in this case might not know, just from the context and the used referring expression, whom the statement is about. But that the hearer does not know this does not show that the statement *was* not about one of these individuals. And in fact the hearer can find out whom the statement was about. So the statement can *be* about one of these individuals in such a case. Hence, in at least some cases it is not context that determines which individual a statement is about, even when the used referring expression applies to—that is, is a name had by or a description satisfied by—more than one individual.

As we have seen, the Context Theory of Referring holds that the sole necessary and sufficient condition of a statement's being about a particular individual rather than any other when the used referring expression applies to more than one individual is that the context in some way indicates that individual. This is its solution to the problem of ambiguous reference. The objection just stated to this proposed solution shows that this is in fact not a necessary condition of such a statement being about a particular individual rather than any other. A statement can be about just one individual rather than any other even though the context does not indicate one individual more than it indicates another. That indication by the context is not a necessary condition of a statement's being about an individual can also be shown in the following way. A speaker's statement can be about a particular individual even in a situation in which there is no relevant context at all. For example, let us suppose that two people meet on the street and begin to talk with one another. The first says "Green is going to Europe

28

next week", where this is the first statement in the conversation. The hearer asks "Who is Green?" The speaker thereupon says "Oh, I thought that you knew Green" and goes on to explain whom it is that his statement was about. It is only after the speaker has said this—that is, has explained whom his statement was about—that the context becomes such as to indicate an individual. But since the speaker is explaining whom his statement *was* about, his statement *was about* this individual *at the time at which the speaker made his statement* and hence prior to the time at which the context became such as to indicate that individual. For the speaker made his statement in the conversation at a time prior to that at which he explained whom his statement was about. Only if the speaker's statement was in fact not about that individual until after the speaker has answered the hearer's question "Who is Green?" would this kind of case not be an objection to the Context Theory of Referring. This theory would have to say that the speaker is explaining, not whom his statement was about, but instead whom he was trying to make a statement about. But this is not what the speaker is doing. Let us suppose that just after the hearer asks "Who is Green?", the conversation is interrupted so that the speaker does not have a chance to answer the hearer's question. And let us also suppose that the speaker and the hearer meet again the following week: the hearer says "I just heard that the Lieutenant Governor of this state is going to Europe this week". The speaker says "But I told you that last week", referring to his earlier statement "Green is going to Europe next week". In saying this the hearer is not denying that the speaker did make a statement last week which was about the Lieutenant Governor of this state. All that the hearer is saying is that he did not know whom that statement was about and hence did not know what the speaker was then trying to tell him. The hearer might even say "Oh, is that what you were saying?" The speaker can truly claim now to have made a statement last week about the Lieutenant Governor. This shows that it is not necessary for the context to indicate one individual rather than any other in order for a statement made by using a referring expression which applies to several individuals to be about just one of those individuals rather than any other.

The first objection set forth above concerns a case in which the context indicates two or more individuals. This type of case cannot show that the context's indicating an individual is not a necessary condition of a statement's being about that individual. For the context in this case does indicate, among others, the individual whom the statement is about. But this is shown by the second objection—that involving a case in which the context indicates no individual at the time at which the statement is made. But the first objection does show that it is not a necessary condition of a statement's being about a particular individual *rather than another* that the context indicate that particular individual *rather than that other*. For in this kind of case, since the context indicates more than one individual, it does not indicate the individual about whom the statement is *rather than* the other individuals whom the statement is not about. And, of course, the second objection shows this also.

4 *Context indication as a sufficient condition of aboutness*

Now let us turn to the question of whether or not an individual's being indicated by the context is a sufficient condition of a statement's being about that individual. If the former were a sufficient condition of the latter, then it would not be possible for a speaker to have made a statement about one individual while the context indicates another individual. But this is possible. Consider the following case. The speaker says "Chaplin is going to Europe next week". On the basis of the context, the hearer believes the speaker is making a statement about a certain lawyer, George Chaplin, whom they had been talking about earlier in the day. But the speaker says that he was making a statement about Charlie Chaplin, the comedian. And he might very well have done so— and did do so if certain conditions to be specified in a later chapter are fulfilled here—even though the context indicates the lawyer instead. Again, if some third person comes up to the speaker and the hearer and says "Charlie Chaplin is going to Europe next week", the first speaker can turn to the hearer and truly say "That's what I said" and "You see, I was right". This shows that what the speaker first said was a statement about Charlie Chaplin.

Thus, the Context Theory of Referring is false. The speaker often does rely on the context to indicate to his hearer whom his statement is about. Thus, he can sometimes use the name 'Wilson' to make a statement about Harold Wilson and be sure that the hearer will know whom he means from the context. But the speaker does not and cannot rely on the context to render his statement a statement about a particular individual. For if context did determine whom a statement is about, the above possible cases would not be possible cases.

IV

THE ABBREVIATION THEORY OF
REFERRING
I

---

1 *Introduction*

In the previous chapter the Context Theory of Referring was found to be unsatisfactory. In this chapter and the next, I will consider a different and widely held theory: that a name or a descriptive phrase which applies to more than one individual can be used to make a statement about *just one particular individual* because the used name is an abbreviation for a description (or, as this is sometimes put, is a disguised description) and because the used description is an abbreviation of a longer description. Thus, the statement "Napoleon was born in 1769" is made by using an expression, 'Napoleon', which is a name of more than one individual. But this statement is about only one of these individuals because, on the theory being discussed, (i) the name 'Napoleon' is an abbreviation of, for example, the descriptive phrase 'the French Emperor who invaded Russia in 1812' and (ii) this descriptive phrase is satisfied by or characterizes one and only one individual, the one whom the statement is then about. There is no difficulty about the statement "The French Emperor who invaded Russia in 1812 was born in 1769" being about just one individual. For only one individual satisfies the referring expression used in making this statement. The difficulty—the problem of ambiguous reference—arises when more than one individual satisfies the used referring expression. And the Abbreviation Theory of Referring attempts to provide an answer to this problem by saying that every statement which is in fact about only one individual but which is made by using a referring expression which apparently applies to more than one individual is in fact identical with a statement which is made by using a referring expression which applies to only one individual. Thus, for example, the statement "Napoleon was born in 1769" would be identical with the statement "The French Emperor who invaded Russia in 1812 was born in 1769". But in order for this to be so, the expression 'Napoleon' must somehow represent or be identical with the expression 'the French Emperor who invaded Russia in 1812'. And what is most often said about this by proponents of this theory is that this name is an abbreviation for this descriptive phrase. This theory is held, with some variations, by Frege,[1] Russell,[2] Quine,[3] Zink,[4] Burks,[5] and Sørensen.[6]

The philosophers just mentioned generally present this theory as a theory about proper names only, and then generally as a theory only about what sort of meaning proper names have. They speak as if their theory were merely a theory about the meaning of proper names rather than a general theory of referring. But it is clear that if proper names do have descriptive meaning by being abbreviations of descriptive phrases, as these people claim, then the above proposed solution to the problem of ambiguous reference follows from this theory about the meaning of names. Moreover, it is clear that exactly the same solution could be proposed about this problem when it arises in connection with descriptive phrases instead of names. For example, it can be said that the reason why the statement "The French Emperor was born in 1769" is about a particular individual, Napoleon, is that the expression 'the French Emperor' is an abbreviation of the expression 'the French Emperor who invaded Russia in 1812' so that this statement is identical with the statement "The French Emperor who invaded Russia in 1812 was born in 1769". For these

[1] *Translations from the Philosophical Writings of Gottlob Frege*, by Peter Geach and Max Black (Blackwell, Oxford, 2nd ed., 1960), p. 58, footnote.
[2] 'The Philosophy of Logical Atomism', *The Monist* (1918), pp. 523-5.
[3] *Methods of Logic* (Holt, 1959), p. 218.
[4] 'The Meaning of Proper Names', *Mind*, LXXII (1963), pp. 481-99.
[5] 'A Theory of Proper Names', *Philosophical Studies*, II (1951), pp. 36-45.
[6] *The Meaning of Proper Names* (G. E. C. Gad, Copenhagen, 1963), pp. 39, 92.

reasons we may call the theory under discussion "The Abbreviation Theory of Referring" rather than merely the "Abbreviation Theory of Names".

What could be meant by saying that a referring expression is an abbreviation of a descriptive phrase? As just noted, one thing that this means is that when the speaker makes a statement by using the referring expression, the statement which he makes is identical with a statement which can be made by using that descriptive phrase. But this is a relation between two statements. What is the relation between the referring expression and the descriptive phrase such that each of these statements is identical with the other? That is, what could the term 'abbreviation' mean when used by proponents of this theory? An abbreviation is generally a linguistic expression which has the same meaning as a longer expression of which the abbreviation is a part. Thus, the letters 'N.Y.' constitute an abbreviation of the expression 'New York'. These letters, when used as such an abbreviation, have whatever meaning the expression 'New York' has; and these letters themselves occur in and as part of the expression 'New York'. Again, the expression 'Gov.' is an abbreviation of the term 'Governor'; the former has the same meaning as and occurs as part of the latter. However, if this is the way in which proponents of this theory are using the term 'abbreviation', then neither names nor descriptive phrases can be regarded as abbreviations of descriptive phrases. For names do not fulfil one of these conditions while descriptive phrases do not fulfil the other. First, the name 'Napoleon' does not in any way occur as part of the descriptive phrase 'the French Emperor who invaded Russia in 1879'. Hence, even if this name does have the same meaning as this descriptive phrase, the name is not properly called an abbreviation of the descriptive phrase.[1] Second, although the descriptive phrase 'the French Emperor' does occur as part of the descriptive phrase 'the French Emperor who invaded Russia in 1812', the former

[1] There is a descriptive phrase in which this name might be said to occur, namely 'the French Emperor who invaded Russia in 1812 and who is named "Napoleon"'. And it might be maintained that a name is an abbreviation of a description only if the description mentions the property of having that name. Even so, the name would not be part of or occur in that description. Instead, it is the name of that name—" 'Napoleon' " instead of 'Napoleon'—which occurs in that description. Hence the name is still not part of what it allegedly abbreviates.

does not have the same meaning as the latter and hence is not properly called an abbreviation of the latter.

In view of this, we could use the term 'abbreviation' as a technical term with the following meaning: "An expression 'X' is an abbreviation of another expression 'Y' if and only if 'X' either has the same meaning as (for the case of names) or is part of (for the case of descriptive phrases) 'Y'". Then if 'Napoleon' did have the same meaning as 'the French Emperor who invaded Russia in 1812', the former would, in this sense of 'abbreviation', be an abbreviation of the latter. And the expression 'the French Emperor' would also be an abbreviation of the latter.

On this view, then, the expression 'Napoleon' has the same meaning as, for example, the description 'the French Emperor who invaded Russia in 1812'. Earlier in this section, it was said that on this theory a speaker who uses the name 'Napoleon' thereby makes a statement which is identical with a statement that can be made by using the expression 'the French Emperor who invaded Russia in 1812'. But what is being said when this is said depends on how the term 'statement' is being used. Let us use the term 'statement' in this book in such a way that two speakers make the same statement if they attribute the same property to the same individual and do not make the same statement if either they attribute different properties to the same individual or they attribute the same property to different individuals or they attribute different properties to different individuals. Thus, if a speaker says "Gordon stamped out the slave trade in the Sudan" (referring successfully to Gordon, the British general, rather than to some other individual) and another speaker says "The hero of Khartoum stamped out the slave trade in the Sudan" (referring successfully to the same person), these two speakers have made the same statement, according to the way in which I will use the term 'statement'. For they have attributed the same property to, and thus said the same thing about, the same individual. 'Making the same statement' thus means "saying the same thing about the same individual". I will use the term 'proposition' in the following way: if two speakers make statements by using sentences which have the same meaning as one another, they have expressed the same proposition even if they have made different statements in so doing. For example, if in 1861 a speaker utters the sentence 'the

D

President of the United States is tall' and in 1966 another speaker utters that same sentence, these speakers have expressed the same proposition but they have made different statements. For the statements which these speakers made were about different individuals. In the first example—the one in which the speakers made the same statement about Gordon of Khartoum by using sentences having different meanings—these speakers made the same statement by expressing different propositions. Now we can say that on the Abbreviation Theory of Referring it is not only the case that when a speaker uses a name he makes the same statement as he would if he had instead used a certain description. He also makes that same statement by expressing the same proposition which he would express if he had instead used that descriptive phrase. For on this theory the name has the same meaning as the descriptive phrase.

If we use the term 'abbreviation' as a technical term in the way indicated previously, we can say that names are abbreviations of descriptive phrases. But there is a serious difficulty with the Abbreviation Theory of Referring as so far described. This difficulty can be put in the following way: if the descriptive phrase 'the French Emperor' is an abbreviation, in this sense of that term, of *every* descriptive phrase of which it is a part, then how on a given occasion can a speaker use this phrase to abbreviate *only one* of the expressions of which it is an abbreviation rather than the others? Why, for example, does a given use of 'the French Emperor' abbreviate the expression 'the French Emperor who invaded Russia in 1812' rather than one of the other expressions of which it is an abbreviation (that is, of which it is a part)? The analogous problem about names can be put in this way: Why on a given occasion is the name 'Napoleon' an abbreviation of one descriptive phrase rather than another? Thus, the Abbreviation Theory of Referring provides a solution for the problem of ambiguous reference, which arises when a referring expression applies to many different individuals, by construing the referring expression as an abbreviation. But then an analogous problem arises with this proposed solution. For the referring expression in question can be an abbreviation of many different descriptive phrases.

This difficulty with the Abbreviation Theory of Referring thus arises with respect to both names and descriptions. Those who claim that names are abbreviations of descriptions generally do not try to deal with this difficulty or with other difficulties associated with this theory. They generally do not describe the theory in any detail. So it is difficult to know how they would deal with these difficulties or even just what their views about names are. What I want to do in the next sections of this chapter is develop this theory (or at least one plausible version of this theory) in detail. I will first do this by considering possible objections to the view that names are abbreviations of descriptions and by showing how this view might, and in some cases must, handle such objections. Most of what I will say in this chapter and the next will be explicitly about names because the thesis that names are synonymous with descriptions is initially more doubtful than the thesis that certain descriptions are parts of other descriptions. But much of what is said here about names will, of course, apply to referring uses of descriptive phrases too. In this way I will try to show just what the Abbreviation Theory of Referring is and to what extent this theory is defensible. Then, in the next group of sections I will discuss some arguments for this theory.

Before embarking on this enterprise, however, a word of warning must be issued. At several points in this chapter and the next, I will make statements asserting or denying that a speaker has succeeded in referring to a particular individual or to any individual at all. These claims depend on certain views on success or lack of success in referring, some of which I develop and defend in discussing the Intention–Description Theory of Referring in later chapters simply because it is far more convenient and natural to do so at that point. So these discussions in the later chapters must be taken into account in evaluating my claims on these points in this chapter and the next.

Now we may proceed to develop the Abbreviation Theory of Referring.

2 *Mentioning properties by using a name*

Every proponent of the view that names are abbreviations of descriptions appears to hold that names have meanings and that each name has the same meaning as some description. It follows from this that when a name is used to refer to an individual, the act of referring is performed in the same way in which it would have been performed if the corresponding description had been used. And presumably this way of referring is by mentioning properties of the individual to whom the speaker is attempting to refer. Thus, for example, when a speaker uses the expression 'the French Emperor who invaded Russia in 1812' to refer successfully to an individual, presumably the speaker thereby mentions some of the properties had by that individual, such as his having been French, his having been an Emperor, his having invaded Russia, and so on. And presumably if a name has the same meaning as a description, then when the speaker uses a name, he refers to the individual in question by mentioning some of the individual's properties in just the way that he does when he uses a description. Only the speaker does not mention these properties explicitly, as in the case of a description. When he uses a name, he mentions properties "implicitly". After all, if the speaker uses the name 'Napoleon', he does not mention properties in the way that he does when he uses the terms 'French' and 'Emperor'. And the way in which he does mention properties can be put by saying that he mentions them "implicitly".

But then, it may be objected, what can possibly be meant by the term 'implicitly' here? What is it to mention properties implicitly and how does this differ from not mentioning properties at all? After all, it seems more likely, *prima facie*, that when a speaker uses a name, he is not mentioning any properties at all. Is it even possible for there to be such a thing as "implicit mention of properties"?

To show that "implicit" mentioning of properties can take place, the Abbreviation Theory of Referring might cite the doctrine that to use a general name, for example, 'chair', is to mention implicitly a group of properties of an object—properties such as "having a seat", "having a back", and so on. It does not matter here whether this doctrine of the mention of properties by the use of general names is true or false. The doctrine is intelligible, even if it turns out to be false. And the intelligibility of this doctrine shows that "implicit mention" of properties is possible. If the use of a general name results in the mention of any properties at all, it must do so implicitly. Certainly the properties of "having a seat", and so on, are not mentioned explicitly when the word 'chair' is used. Since implicit mention of properties is a possible function, the Abbreviation Theory of Referring is justified, to this extent at least, in saying that there is implicit mention of properties in the use of a proper name.

3 The specificity of names and descriptions

It might now be objected that names cannot be used to refer to individuals in the way in which descriptions can be used because names and descriptions have different properties in their referring role. For one thing, a name is used to refer to only one individual at a time, whereas a descriptive referring phrase can characterize and fit more than one individual at a time. But this is not correct. A name which is used to refer successfully to just one individual can be the name of many individuals. And descriptive phrases which do fit many individuals—such as the description 'The Senator' which fits every individual who is a Senator—can nevertheless be used on a given occasion to refer to just one of the individuals whom it fits. The analogue to a description's fitting many individuals is a name's *being* a name of many individuals, not the name's being used to refer to just one individual.

4 The results of giving a name to an individual

There is, nevertheless, a very important difference between names and descriptions, the objector might say. It seems to be an essential property of a proper name that it must have been *given* to a particular individual in order to be, first, a name of that individual and, second, usable to refer successfully to that individual. Since being given to an individual is an essential element in being able to refer successfully to that individual in the case of names but not in the case of descriptions, names are used in referring in a way in which descriptions are not used. Or, rather, the use of names results in successful reference in a way different from that in which the use of descriptive phrases does so. In fact, those who would urge this objection to the theory being discussed might also say that in giving a name to an individual, one makes it possible to refer to that individual, not by mentioning that individual's properties, but in a more direct, non-descriptive, quasi-ostensive way. These people would probably say that referring by the use of a name is in some ways like pointing to the individual and hence very different from using a description or mentioning the individual's properties.

However, this does not show that names are used to refer in a non-descriptive way, that is, without implicitly mentioning properties of the individual being referred to. For on the Abbreviation Theory of Referring, the giving of a name can be regarded as *the operation of making that name an abbreviation of certain descriptive phrases*. A name is an abbreviation for certain descriptions and not for others. By giving a name to an individual, the speaker renders that name an abbreviation of one or more of the descriptive phrases which characterize that particular individual. Giving a name sets up the relation of abbreviation between that name and certain descriptions. Therefore, that names must be given does not show that names are not abbreviations of descriptive phrases. In fact, that names must be given is just what would be expected on the theory that names are such abbreviations. For the relations between an abbreviation and what it abbreviates must be set up in some way, particularly where the abbreviation is to be used in communication among individuals as proper names are generally used.

It should be pointed out that what was just said is relevant to and part of an answer to the difficulty raised at the end of Section 1 of this chapter. The difficulty, as it arose in connection with names, was there put in this way: "Why on a given occasion is the name 'Napoleon' an abbreviation of one descriptive phrase rather than another?" What is said above does not completely answer this question. But what is said above does at least limit the class of descriptions of which a name can be an abbreviation. According to what is said above, a necessary condition of a name's being an abbreviation of a descriptive phrase is that that descriptive phrase characterize some individual to whom that name has been given. Moreover, since, according to the Abbreviation Theory of Referring, names are used as abbreviations of uniquely characterizing descriptions—that is, descriptions that characterize, either contingently or necessarily, only one individual at a time—the following can be said: A necessary condition of a name's being an abbreviation of a descriptive phrase is that that descriptive phrase *uniquely* characterize some individual to whom that name has been given. This is by no means a complete answer to the question that was asked at the end of Section 1 of this chapter. For there still may be many descriptions which uniquely characterize the individuals to whom the name 'Napoleon' has been given. And so it must still be said which of these the name 'Napoleon' abbreviates when that name is used to make a statement on a particular occasion.

It should be pointed out that whatever the descriptions abbreviated by a given name, these descriptions cannot all be associated with the giving of the name. That is, if the name 'Napoleon' is given to an individual by his father, Carlo Buonaparte, it cannot be the case that the one and only description abbreviated by the name 'Napoleon' (at least with respect to this Napoleon) is the description 'the individual who was given the name "Napoleon" by Carlo Buonaparte'. And this is not because the name 'Napoleon' cannot itself be mentioned in a description which that name abbreviates. In fact, as we shall see, that name may be mentioned in every such description. Instead, this cannot be the only description abbreviated by the name 'Napoleon' because a speaker can correctly use the name 'Napoleon' to make a statement about the individual in question and yet not know who gave this individual his name 'Napoleon'. On the theory being discussed, names have meanings. And presumably, also on this theory, when a speaker uses a name correctly, he knows what the meaning of that name is. But it is often not the case that a speaker who correctly uses a proper name knows who gave the individual being referred to that name. Hence, it cannot be the case that the only description abbreviated by a name is of the type described above. Nor is it the case, for reasons of exactly the same sort, that the only descriptions abbreviated by a name are those connected with the giving of the name in other ways—for example, which mention the time and place at which the name was given—or which mention such facts about the individual as the time and place of his birth, the names of his parents, and so on. For it is possible that a speaker correctly uses this name to refer to this individual and yet does not know when and where the individual was born, who his parents were, and so on. This shows that whatever the descriptions are that are abbreviated by a certain name, it must be possible for these descriptions to mention properties of many different types, not just those associated with, for example, the giving of that name to that individual.

This is connected with another and very important thesis which must be maintained by the Abbreviation Theory of Referring. Let us suppose that the speaker uses the name 'Malraux' to make the following statement about an individual: "Malraux created a new literary form in writing his memoirs". On the theory being discussed, the speaker thereby makes a statement identical with one which could be made by using a certain descriptive referring phrase. But that statement—the one made by using the descriptive phrase—will be about that particular individual only because that descriptive phrase uniquely characterizes that individual *at the time at which that statement is made*. If in 1968 a speaker made the statement "The present President of the Chamber of Deputies is a Gaullist" with the intention of saying something about André Malraux, he would not succeed in doing so. For the descriptive phrase 'the present President of the Chamber of Deputies' does not characterize Malraux at all, let alone uniquely, in 1968. Thus, it must be possible for a name to abbreviate, among others, descriptions which uniquely characterize the individual in question at any point in time, at least any time after the individual is given that name. For if an individual has been given a name, it is possible to use that name at any moment thereafter to refer successfully to that individual. This is not to say that a name must abbreviate a single description which uniquely characterizes that individual at every moment after the individual is given that name. Instead, it is to say that if an individual has been given a name, then given any moment thereafter, there must be at least one description which uniquely characterizes that individual at that moment and which it is possible for the name to abbreviate.

5 *Names as ambiguous words*

On the theory being considered, it is possible for a name to be an abbreviation of more than one description at the same time. That this is possible on this theory can be shown in the following way.

Two individuals can have the name 'John'; and a speaker can refer successfully to either of these individuals by using that name. Let us suppose that Jones uses 'John' to refer to one of these individuals and that at the same time Smith uses 'John' to refer to the other individual. On the Abbreviation Theory of Referring, each speaker succeeds in referring to one or the other of these individuals because the name which he uses is an abbreviation of a description which uniquely characterizes the individual to whom he succeeds in referring. But these two speakers succeed in referring to two different individuals. Hence it must be the case in this situation that two different descriptions are being abbreviated. For if the name 'John' as used by each speaker abbreviated exactly the same description, only one and the same individual—the one uniquely characterized by that one description—would be successfully referred to in the two cases. But two different individuals are referred to successfully here and by the use of one and the same name 'John'. Hence the one name 'John' must be an abbreviation for at least two different descriptions. Consequently, it is possible, on this theory, for a name to be an abbreviation of at least two different descriptions at the same time.

But it follows from this that on this theory it is possible for a name to have more than one meaning at the same time. For on this theory a name has the same meaning as that description of which it is an abbreviation, and it is possible for a name to be an abbreviation of more than one description at the same time. Words which have more than one meaning are said to be "ambiguous". Hence, on this theory it is possible for a name to be ambiguous in just the same way as a word of any other sort may be ambiguous.

6 Referring to an individual about whom the speaker knows only that individual's name

Next, the following objection might be raised. It is possible for a speaker to use a name to refer to an individual without knowing anything about the individual to whom he is trying to refer except that that individual has that name. Let us suppose that the name in question is 'Wilcox'. Then, in such a case the speaker is trying to refer to whoever it is that has the name 'Wilcox'. Since the speaker knows nothing at all about this individual except his name, the speaker is not using an expression which is an abbreviation for a description here. As said before, a speaker who uses a name correctly and thereby succeeds in referring to an individual presumably knows what the meaning of that name is, if that name has a meaning. But in the case just described, the speaker successfully refers to an individual and yet does not know what any of that individual's properties are except that that individual has a certain name. So the Abbreviation Theory of Referring must say in this case either that (i) the name has a descriptive meaning but the speaker does not know what that meaning is because he does not know what properties that individual has, or (ii) in this case the name is not an abbreviation of a description. If this theory asserted (i), then it would be admitted by the theory that a speaker can correctly use a name to refer successfully to an individual and yet not know what the meaning of that name is.

But in fact it is not necessary for this theory to assert either (i) or (ii). Let us assume that it is possible for a speaker to refer successfully to an individual by using the name 'Wilcox' even though the speaker does not know what any of the properties of this individual are. The speaker may not even know that the property which he is predicating of that individual does in fact belong to that individual, for the statement which he makes about that individual may be false. In this sort of case, a proponent of the Abbreviation Theory of Referring can hold that *the description which the name 'Wilcox' here abbreviates is: 'the individual named "Wilcox"* '. That is, in such a case as this, the speaker does use the name as an abbreviation of a description where that description mentions only the property of having that name itself. It follows from this that the speaker will succeed in referring to an individual in such a case as this only if it is the case that there is one and only one individual who has the name which the speaker uses in making his statement. For example, only if there is one and only one individual named 'Wilcox' will this speaker succeed in referring to an individual. For the abbreviated description must, according to this theory, uniquely characterize an individual. And a description which mentions only one property uniquely characterizes an individual only if there is one and only one individual who has that property.

7 *Names as abbreviations of descriptions at a given time*

It might now be objected that if a name is given to an individual who satisfies a certain descriptive phrase and the name thereby becomes an abbreviation of the descriptive phrase, then the name can be used to refer successfully to any individual who satisfies that description even if this latter individual does not have—that is, has never been given—that name. If the name has a certain meaning by being made an abbreviation of a certain description, the name can, on this theory, be used to refer successfully to any individual who satisfies that description regardless of any other properties that individual may or may not have, including the individual's having or not having that name, since the description may be so used. But, as we shall see in discussing the Intention–Description Theory of Referring, a name in fact cannot be used to refer successfully to an individual who does not have that name (unless, perhaps, the name is not a name of that individual but instead someone's name for that individual). Hence, names are not abbreviations of descriptions.

As an example, the objector might give the following. Let us suppose that at time t_1 the name 'Jones' is given to an individual who uniquely satisfies the description 'the individual in Room 1512 of the Empire State Building'. And let us suppose that the name 'Jones' becomes in this way an abbreviation for the description just mentioned. But then this individual leaves Room 1512 of the Empire State Building and at a later time t_2 a different individual becomes the individual who uniquely satisfies that description. The name 'Jones' has, on the theory being considered, the same meaning as does the description 'the individual in Room 1512 of the Empire State Building'. And since this description uniquely characterizes this individual at time t_2, this description can be used to refer successfully to this second individual at time t_2. But then so can the name 'Jones', since the name 'Jones' has the same meaning as that description. Consequently, the name 'Jones' can, on this theory, be used to refer successfully to an individual, namely the second individual, who does not have the name 'Jones' even though the name 'Jones' is an abbreviation of a description which uniquely characterizes an individual.

There are at least two replies which the Abbreviation Theory of

Referring can make to this objection. The first reply is this. Whatever description the name 'Jones' abbreviates, that description mentions, among other properties, the property of having the name 'Jones'. Thus, the name 'Napoleon' does not abbreviate the description 'the French Emperor who invaded Russia in 1812' but instead the description 'the French Emperor who invaded Russia in 1812 and who was named "Napoleon"'. Then the name 'Napoleon' presumably could not be used to refer successfully to any individual who was not named 'Napoleon'. And the name 'Jones' could not be used to refer successfully at time t_2 to the second individual in the case described in the preceding paragraph, since the second individual does not have the name 'Jones'. It should be noticed that the description abbreviated by a name in a case (see Section 6 of this chapter) in which the speaker is referring to whoever has that name—namely the description 'the individual named "Wilcox"', where 'Wilcox' is the used name—is a limiting case, on this view, of the sort of description usually abbreviated by names; the former mentions only the property of having a certain name while the descriptions usually abbreviated mention other properties in addition to the having of a certain name.

One difficulty with this reply, however, is that it is possible that a description can apply to or characterize an individual even though that individual does not have every one of the properties mentioned in the description. If so, then a description which mentioned the property of having a certain name, as well as other properties, could uniquely characterize, and thus be usable to refer successfully to, an individual even though that individual did not have that name.

The second reply that could be given to this objection by the Abbreviation Theory of Referring is this. A name does not abbreviate a certain description. Instead, a name abbreviates a certain description *at a certain time*. Thus, there is no such thing as the group of descriptions which a given name abbreviates. Instead, there is only the group of descriptions which a name abbreviates at a given time. And this group can (and usually will) have different members from moment to moment. A name abbreviates at time t_1 all or some of those descriptions which one of the individuals who had that name uniquely satisfies at t_1. Since some of an individual's properties change from one time to another, the group of descriptions abbreviated by a given name will usually change from one time to another. On this view, the second individual in the case described above could not be referred to by the use of the name 'Jones'. For since that second individual is not named 'Jones', there is no description that the name 'Jones' abbreviates and which uniquely characterizes that second individual. The name 'Jones' abbreviates at time t_2 only those descriptions which uniquely characterize some individual who has the name 'Jones' at time t_2. Thus, at time t_2 the name 'Jones' no longer abbreviates the description 'the individual in Room 1512 of the Empire State Building' and hence that name cannot be used at time t_2 to refer successfully to the second individual.

Since this second reply seems more adequate than the first reply—the first reply being subject to the difficulty mentioned earlier in this section—we will henceforth in this chapter regard names as abbreviations of changing sets of descriptions or as being abbreviations of a set of descriptions *at a given time.*

8 *Acquiring a name by satisfying a description*

An objection which is similar to that discussed in Section 7 might be made at this point. It might be said that on this theory if a name is given to an individual who satisfies a certain description, then that name is had by any individual who also satisfies that description or who later comes to satisfy that description in place of the individual to whom the name was given. But in fact names cannot be acquired by individuals in this way. The second individual does not come to have the name 'Jones' just because he comes to satisfy the description 'the individual in Room 1512 of the Empire State Building'. Consequently, the Abbreviation Theory of Referring is incorrect.

We may reply to this objection in the same way in which we replied to the previous objection. If the set of descriptions which a name abbreviates changes over time, then it is not possible at time t_2 to refer successfully to the second individual by using the name 'Jones'. For the name 'Jones' no longer abbreviates the description 'the individual in Room 1512 of the Empire State Building'. And hence there is no basis for saying that on this theory at time t_2 the name 'Jones' becomes a name of that second individual. So the thesis that an individual can acquire a name only by being given that name is compatible with the Abbreviation Theory of Referring.

Thus, on the version of the Abbreviation Theory of Referring which I am setting forth here, a name comes to be an abbreviation of a description by having a certain relation to an individual who satisfies that description, usually by having been given to that individual. The individual is in this respect the intermediary between the name and the description. A name is first of all given to an individual and in this way comes to stand for certain descriptive phrases. The name goes along with or follows the individual, not the descriptive phrase. It does not first come to stand for certain descriptive phrases and in this way come to be the name of the individuals uniquely characterized by those descriptive phrases. The relation between a name and a description is dependent on the existence of a relationship between the name and an individual. It is then usually changes in the relation between the individual and descriptive phrases—the individual ceasing to satisfy certain phrases and coming to satisfy other phrases—that produces changes in what descriptions a name abbreviates. (Of course, this can also be produced by an individual's coming to have or ceasing to have that name.) On the Abbreviation Theory of Referring, having a certain name is a property which an individual has in virtue (usually) of having been given that name and not in virtue of satisfying certain descriptions (unless a description has been used in giving that name, as in "Let the name of the individual now in Room 1512 of the Empire State Building be 'John' ").

On the theory being presented, names differ from descriptions in several ways. Properties are mentioned explicitly by the use of descriptions but implicitly by the use of names. (See Section 2 of this chapter.) Names apparently must be given to individuals in order to have meanings, while this is not so for descriptions. Names are in this way like code words. A code word has the same meaning, *qua* code word, as that which it encodes. And the giving of a name is, as far as the acquiring of meaning by a name is concerned, analogous to the setting up of a code. Names generally change their meanings when individuals change their properties, while the meaning of a description is independent of what properties this or that particular individual possesses. This is perhaps why it seems to some to be incorrect to say that names have meanings. In the case of other types of expressions, the meaning of the expression is independent of the state of the world in the sense that an expression can have what meaning it has regardless of what properties any particular individual has. But this is not so for names, on the theory being presented. On this theory a name at time t_1 has as one of its meanings the meaning of each descriptive phrase which at that time uniquely characterizes an individual to whom that name has been given.

9 *Hearer-identification on the Abbreviation Theory of Referring*

It is not an objection to the Abbreviation Theory of Referring that a hearer can believe that the speaker is using a name which abbreviates a description 'Ø' which is different from the description 'Θ' which that name in fact abbreviates, and yet still identifies correctly the individual to whom the speaker succeeds in referring because 'Ø' and 'Θ' happen to be uniquely satisfied by one and the same individual. For in claiming that names abbreviate descriptions, this theory is not claiming that the hearer will always know which description the used name abbreviates, even when the hearer correctly identifies the individual being referred to. That is, this theory does not claim that the hearer will identify the correct individual only if the hearer knows which description the uttered name abbreviates. (On this topic, see also Section 6 of Chapter V.)

It should also be pointed out here that the descriptive phrase which the speaker utters in answer to the question "Whom do you mean?" or "To whom are you referring?" is not necessarily the descriptive phrase which the name that the speaker used abbreviates. The descriptive phrase which he utters in answer to this may be only part of the abbreviated descriptive phrase. For what the speaker says in answer to this question may well be determined in part by what the speaker believes about the hearer, and in particular by what the speaker believes about what will lead the hearer to identify the correct individual as the one being referred to by the speaker. For this reason, the speaker might utter one part rather than another part of the abbreviated description in answer to this question. The speaker might also use a descriptive phrase to answer this question where that descriptive phrase is *not at all* the one abbreviated by the name at the time at which he used the name. For the name may have changed its meaning in the way described in Section 7, so that the description which the name abbreviated when the name was used to make that statement is no longer abbreviated by that name and instead other descriptions are now abbreviated by that name. And the speaker might have to use one of these other descriptions to lead the hearer to identify the correct individual as the individual to whom the speaker was referring.

10 *Using the same name to refer to two different individuals*

Kenny objects to the Abbreviation Theory of Referring in the following way:

> For this reason, I would not wish to say, as Russell did of ordinary names, and as Quine suggests of names in general, that a name is an abbreviated definite description. For two different speakers, if they use a name to refer to the same person, use the name with the same meaning; but the definite description by which one speaker identifies the person named may be wholly different from that by which the other speaker identifies him.[1]

What Kenny seems to mean here is this: the name has the same meaning in each of the two cases; but if the name abbreviates a description at all, it abbreviates a different description in each case; therefore neither description can be identical with the meaning of the name.

This objection is not sound. There is no reason why one and the same name cannot *have* two different meanings at one and the same time. We have already said that the Abbreviation Theory of Referring must hold that names can be ambiguous, just as words of other types can (see Section 5). And in the sort of case described by Kenny, the name in question is ambiguous in just this way.

[1] A. Kenny, 'Oratio Obliqua', *Aristotelian Society Supplementary Volume*, XXXVII (1963), p. 140.

It may perhaps be replied: "But this name is not ambiguous; the name would be ambiguous only if the name had more than one meaning; but since the name is in each case used to refer successfully to one and the same individual, that name has only one meaning". After all, it is maintained in the above quotation that if the two speakers "use a name to refer to the same person, they use the name with the same meaning". Thus the following principle seems to be employed here: "The meaning of a referring expression on a given occasion is determined by which individual that expression is used to refer to on that occasion". But this principle is false. For if this principle were correct, then if two speakers used the same *descriptive referring expression*—for example, the description 'the Director of the Bank of Greece'—to refer successfully to two different individuals (as when one speaker utters this expression in 1887 and the other in 1964), this expression would have two different meanings on these two occasions, one meaning on the first occasion and another meaning on the second occasion. But this is not so. The expression 'the Director of the Bank of Greece' has one and the same meaning on every occasion on which it is used, although it may be used to refer to different individuals on these different occasions. Therefore, the above principle is false.

It may then be said that this apparent counterexample to the principle is not in fact a counterexample because it involves a descriptive referring expression whereas the principle is intended to apply only to names. But this reply assumes that names are in fact quite different from descriptive referring expressions. Yet this is exactly what is at issue here. What the objector is trying to show is that names are quite different from descriptive referring expressions—that names are not abbreviations of and hence do not have the same meaning as descriptive referring expressions. Since this is what he is trying to show, he cannot say that his principle applies only to names and not also to descriptive referring expressions unless he has *already* shown in some *other* way that names are quite different from descriptive referring expressions. And if he had shown this in some other way, he would not need to employ this principle. Since the objector does employ this principle without showing this in some other way, his objection to the Abbreviation Theory of Referring is not sound.

11 *Using a name in one of its meanings*

Now let us consider a somewhat different case from that just discussed, namely a case in which two speaker use the same name to refer to two *different* individuals. There *is* a difference between what the first speaker does and what the second speaker does when they use exactly the same name to refer to different individuals. Clearly, there must be such a difference in order to allow the two speakers to refer to different individuals.

It appears that the Abbreviation Theory of Referring must account for this difference in the following way. Typically a name will have more than one meaning. That is, typically a name is ambiguous. When a name is given to an individual, that name becomes an abbreviation for each of the descriptive referring phrases that uniquely characterize that individual. And at each later moment t_1 the name is an abbreviation for whatever descriptive referring phrases uniquely characterize that individual (and any other individual who has been given that name) at t_1, as was stated in Section 7. So at any given time a certain name is likely to be an abbreviation of more than one descriptive phrase even if that name has been given to only one individual, because it is likely that at that moment there is more than one descriptive phrase which uniquely characterizes that individual.

How can a name which is not only ambiguous but also a name of more than one individual be used to refer to just one of those individuals? The name can be used to do this in exactly the same way in which an ambiguous word of another sort can be used to make a single statement. Consider the following sentence: 'The gauge moved when George slammed the door'. This sentence can be used to make either one of two different statements. When the speaker utters this sentence, he can be making either the statement "The gauge indicated a different measurement at the same time that George slammed the door" (that is, the needle moved) or the statement "The gauge moved on its resting place when George slammed the door" (that is, the whole gauge, case and all, moved). Here the expression 'the gauge moved' is ambiguous. Another example is this: one soldier says to another "Let's mark this spot as a location for a post". Here the soldier could be talking about a sentry post or about a fence post. The word 'post' is ambiguous. But in each case the speaker can make one or the other of these statements by using the ambiguous word or expression. When the speaker does so, he is employing only one of the meanings of the ambiguous word or phrase. The soldier, for example, means either 'sentry post' or 'fence post'.[1] When the speaker *means* one of the several meanings that an ambiguous word has, we will say that the speaker is *using* that word *in* one of its meanings. It should be noticed that which meaning a word is used in is not determined by the sentence in which that word occurs but rather by the speaker himself, at least in many cases. For the whole sentence itself may be ambiguous, as in the case in both of the examples given above, and so cannot help to fix the meaning of one of its constituent terms.

Thus, an ambiguous word can be used *in* just one of its meanings even though that word has several different meanings. The Abbreviation Theory of Referring must say that when a speaker uses a name that has several different meanings and moreover the name is had by several different individuals, and the speaker uses that name to refer to just one individual, the speaker is using that name *in* just one of its meanings. When a name is used *in* a meaning which is the meaning of a certain descriptive phrase, we will say that the name is being used to *stand for* that descriptive phrase. In every case in which the speaker uses an ambiguous name *in* a meaning, it is the speaker himself alone who determines what meaning he is using that ambiguous name in. For every sentence in which an ambiguous name which is a name of more than one individual occurs is an ambiguous sentence. It is a sentence that can be used to make several different statements—at least as many statements as there are individuals who have that name. Such a sentence can be used to make a statement about each one of these individuals. And since the individuals are different from one another, each of these statements will be different from one another. Since the sentence in which the name occurs is ambiguous in this way, the sentence does not determine which meaning the name is being used in. Nor does the context determine this, for

[1] He could mean both at once, perhaps, particularly if the way they are using to indicate that a sentry post should be established in a certain location is by putting a fence post in that location.

reasons very similar to the reasons which are given in Chapter III. It is the speaker himself who determines in which meaning an ambiguous name is being used by him on a given occasion.

Thus, when two speakers use the same name to refer to different individuals, it is not that the name *has* one meaning when used by one speaker and another meaning when used by the other speaker. Instead, the name *has* the *same* meanings when used by each speaker, but each speaker *uses* that name *in* a different one of the meanings which that name *has*.

When a speaker uses a name in a particular case to make a statement, he may be said to use a 'token' of that name. If many speakers use tokens of the same name all at the same time, those tokens all *have* the same meaning. But each token may be *used in* a different one of those meanings. It is tokens which are used *in* this or that meaning. Names are used *in* this or that meaning only in so far as their tokens are used in this or that meaning. It may be possible for a speaker to use a given token in two of its meanings at one and the same time. If this is possible, then a speaker can make two statements at once by uttering one sentence. For example, the speaker could say that two different men are tall by uttering the sentence 'John is tall'. For he could be using this token of 'John' in two of its meanings. As we will see in the discussion of the Intention–Description Theory of Referring, there is nothing in the notion of "using a word in one of its meanings" which prevents a token from being used in more than one of its meanings at the same time.

12 *Arguments for the correctness of this theory*

This completes the development of the Abbreviation Theory of Referring that I think is necessary to make it a plausible theory, one which may be capable of accounting for the varied phenomena of referring. The chief features of this theory are: its explanation of what it is for a name or description to be an abbreviation; its claim that a name or a description is an abbreviation of a set of descriptions where this set changes its membership through time as individuals gain and lose properties; the view that a name has the same meanings as the descriptions which it abbreviates and that a token of a name can be used *in* one of these meanings on a given occasion; similarly, a token of a description can be used to stand for just one of the descriptions of which it is an abbreviation. I have tried to show just which facts about the activity of referring these features of the theory are intended to account for. Now I wish to present and discuss some arguments for the correctness of this theory.

The best reasons for believing that this version of the theory is correct are these. First, this theory provides a satisfactory solution for the problem of ambiguous reference as set forth in Chapter I. How can a speaker refer to one particular individual by using a referring expression which applies to more than one individual? The answer given by this theory is that the speaker uses the expression in just one of its meanings or to stand for just one of the descriptions which it abbreviates. Second, if the speaker is asked "To whom are you referring?" he will either at first or ultimately use a descriptive phrase to answer this question (even if the description is only of the form 'the only individual to have the name "N"'). And this provides a reason for believing that this descriptive phrase is at least not unconnected with the use of the name. Third, names seem to behave in just the same way that ambiguous words do when those names are the names of more than one individual. It is, in both cases, the speaker who is the final authority on which statement he made by uttering what he uttered when there is more than one statement which he could have been making. In the case of an ambiguous word, the speaker uses the word in one of its meanings. Since he is the one who determines what meaning the word is used in, he is the one who determines which of the possible statements he did in fact make. And it is the case that when a speaker uses a name which is a name of more than one individual, the speaker is the one who determines which statement (in our sense of 'statement') he made—in particular, which individual he referred to. This is evidence for the thesis that a name which is a name of more than one individual is a word which has more than one meaning and that the speaker uses that name in one of its meanings. But if this thesis is true, then a name has meanings. The only candidates for the meanings of names are the meanings of descriptive phrases. For only these would allow the speaker to use a name to pick out one individual in the way in which he does by using a name. Consequently, it seems that the meanings of names are identical with the meanings of descriptive referring phrases. Similar, though not identical, things can be said about "ambiguous descriptions"—descriptions which apply to more than one individual.

13 *Meaningful symbols which are grammatical subjects but do not denote individuals*

Another possible argument for this theory is as follows. Let us suppose that a speaker uses a sentence containing a symbol that has no connotation. The sentence contains this symbol in the grammatical subject position of the sentence. The speaker uses this symbol in an attempt to refer to an individual. But there is no individual of which this symbol is a name. If there is no individual (existing, mythological, and so on) having the properties which the speaker believes the individual whom he believes to have this symbol as a name to possess, then it would be said that the speaker had not succeeded in referring to anyone. But it would not be said that what the speaker said was meaningless. Yet an utterance is meaningful only if all of its component parts are meaningful. Therefore, the symbol which occupies the position of grammatical subject in this sentence must be meaningful. But the meaning of this symbol cannot be identical with an individual, as is sometimes claimed about proper names. For whatever it may mean to say that the meaning of a name is an individual, it is clear that for a symbol to have an individual as its meaning, there must be some individual which can serve as that meaning. And there is no such individual in this case. It seems that the only possible meaning that this symbol could have is a descriptive meaning.

This argument does perhaps give some support to the theory that names have descriptive meanings and hence to the Abbreviation Theory of Referring. But to provide conclusive support for this theory, it would have to be shown that such a symbol could not be used referentially in some way which did not involve the symbol's having a descriptive meaning even though the speaker was attempting to refer to an individual who, if he had existed, could have been successfully referred to by the use of a certain descriptive phrase.

14 *Names and existence statements*

Suppose that a speaker says "Napoleon never existed" or "There was no such individual as Napoleon". Again, what the speaker says is meaningful. Hence the term 'Napoleon' is meaningful. But if what the speaker says is true, then this term cannot have some sort of ostensive meaning. For there is no individual to be pointed to here. Hence this term must have a descriptive meaning. That this term has a descriptive meaning can be shown in the following way too. The speaker who makes this statement would not regard what he said as false if he found that there was *some* individual or other who existed and was named 'Napoleon'. He would regard his statement as false only if he found that there was a *certain* individual—an individual with certain particular properties—who existed and was named 'Napoleon'. Thus, the term 'Napoleon' which he uses has descriptive import.

Even if this does show that the token of 'Napoleon' which this speaker uses does have descriptive import, this argument might be regarded as not relevant to the theory of referring. For this speaker is not using this token to *refer* to an individual. After all, the speaker not only believes that there is no such individual but is in fact using this term to deny that there is such an individual. Consequently, he cannot be trying to refer to an individual. Thus, what is true about this case shows nothing about the meanings of tokens that are used to refer to individuals.

But it might be objected that if the speaker says "Napoleon never existed" and what he says is false, then what he said was about a particular individual. He said of an individual who existed that that individual did not exist. Hence what he said was about that individual. But if what he said was about that individual, then he did refer to that individual. For we are using the term 'refer' in such a way that if a statement is about a particular individual, then the speaker has referred to that individual (even though he may not have been attempting to refer to that individual and hence did not succeed in referring to that individual). So what the speaker says, when he says "Napoleon never existed", can be relevant to the theory of referring and is so relevant when what he says is false. But the meaning or import of the term 'Napoleon' does not depend on whether or not what the speaker says is true or false.

Therefore, since this term has descriptive meaning when the statement is true, this term has descriptive meaning when the statement is false and the speaker has referred to an individual. Hence, this term has descriptive meaning when the speaker refers to an individual by using this term. This shows that in some cases of reference referring expressions have descriptive meaning.

15 *Saying what can be said by the use of a name by using a description*

It might be said that the fact that every statement that can be made by using a name can also be made by using a descriptive phrase shows that names have the same meanings as descriptions.

But this is not a good argument for this theory. For the argument could equally well go in the other direction. That is, it might also be said that every statement that can be made by using a descriptive phrase could in principle be made by using a name—provided that every individual there is had been given a name. And what this might show is that the meaning of a descriptive referring phrase is irrelevant to the referring use of a name. It might be claimed that the fact that this is possible shows that descriptive meaning is not involved in referring at all, that descriptive phrases made reference possible in just the way in which names did, and that since names do not have meanings, descriptive phrases are not usable to refer to individuals in virtue of their meaning but instead in virtue of some other property which they possess.

16 *Using a name which is not the name of the individual in question*

Suppose that a speaker believes that a certain individual has the name 'Clark', whereas that individual does not have the name 'Clark' and instead has the name 'Stanley'. The speaker also believes that Stanley is in New York and so says "Clark is in New York". The hearer knows whom the speaker is talking about, knows that Stanley is not in New York, and knows that Stanley does not have the name 'Clark'. But the hearer says "Clark is not in New York". Since the hearer knows that 'Clark' is not the name of the individual in question, the hearer cannot be using the name 'Clark' to refer in some ostensive or non-descriptive way to Stanley. Hence, the hearer must be using 'Clark' to refer to Stanley in a descriptive way. He must be using 'Clark' as an abbreviation for a description which is uniquely satisfied by Stanley.

But this is not so. The hearer does not succeed in referring to Stanley at all, let alone by using a name in a certain descriptive meaning. For, as we will see in Chapter VI, the term 'Clark' cannot be used to refer successfully to an individual none of whose names is 'Clark' (unless 'Clark' is someone's name for that individual). The hearer has conveyed information about Stanley to the speaker but he has not done so by referring to Stanley. The hearer has only referred the speaker to Stanley, not referred to Stanley. The distinction between referring to an individual and referring a hearer to an individual will be discussed further in Chapter VI.

17 *Names which are not the grammatical subjects of sentences*

There are certain statements in the making of which a proper name seems to be used predicatively and thus in a way in which a descriptive phrase might be used. Geach cites Frege's example: "Trieste is no Vienna", and claims that 'Vienna' is not a proper name here. Geach says "A proper name is never used predicatively—unless it ceases to be a proper name, as in . . . 'Trieste is no Vienna'; in such cases the word alludes to certain attributes of the object customarily designated by the proper name".[1] Presumably Geach means that the statement "Trieste is no Vienna" is identical with some such statement as "Trieste is not a city which has properties $\emptyset$, Θ, and so on", where $\emptyset$, Θ, and so on are notable properties of Vienna. But Geach does not say why "Trieste is no Vienna" cannot be construed as identical with some such statement as "Trieste is not similar to Vienna", where 'Vienna' is used as a name to refer to the city.

In either case, however, the existence of such statements as "Trieste is no Vienna", in which a proper name appears in the predicate of the sentence used to make the statement, does not provide support for the Abbreviation Theory of Referring. First, let us suppose that in this statement the term 'Vienna' is used to

[1] P. T. Geach, *Reference and Generality* (Cornell University Press, Ithaca, 1962), p. 42.

allude to certain properties. If this is correct, then 'Vienna' might be said to have a descriptive meaning of a certain sort. But nevertheless, if Geach is correct, then 'Vienna' is not being used to refer to an individual here. So that 'Vienna' does have a descriptive meaning in this case does not show that a proper name has a descriptive meaning *when that name is used to refer to an individual.* For, if Geach is correct, this is not a case in which 'Vienna' is used to refer to an individual (in this case, to a city). Now let us suppose that 'Vienna' is here used to refer to the city and hence to an individual. But now there is no reason to construe the name as "alluding" to properties and hence there is no reason to believe that the name has a descriptive meaning in this use. Hence, in neither case can the existence of such statements support the Abbreviation Theory of Referring.

V

THE ABBREVIATION THEORY OF
REFERRING
II

1 *Introduction*

The Abbreviation Theory of Referring has been developed and defended in Chapter IV. In this chapter I shall consider several important objections to this theory and discuss two particular versions of it.

2 *Another type of descriptive phrase that may be abbreviated by a name*

Searle raises the following important objection to the Abbreviation Theory of Referring. Let us suppose that the name 'Napoleon' is being used in a certain case *in* its meaning 'the French Emperor who was born in 1769, who was an artillery officer in the French army, and who invaded Russia in 1812'. Searle claims that if the name was used in this meaning,[1] that is, if this name was used as synonymous with this description, then the speaker would succeed in referring to an individual only if that individual had every single property mentioned in that descriptive phrase. But it could be found that, for example, Napoleon was in fact born in 1768 instead of 1769. And yet, even though Napoleon thus did not have one

---

[1] He does not talk about 'using a name in a certain meaning'—that is our doctrine, not one which he attributes to the theory being discussed—but this is how this objection would have to be put in order for it to apply to the version of the Abbreviation Theory of Referring which I am developing here.

of the properties mentioned in the abbreviated description, we could still correctly say that the speaker had succeeded in referring to Napoleon. This shows that the name 'Napoleon' is not an abbreviation of a description and that names are never abbreviations of descriptive phrases. Searle claims that this also shows that the relation between names and descriptive phrases is this: the use of a name "presupposes" that a certain number of descriptive phrases characterize (and presumably this means that some set of these descriptive phrases uniquely characterize) an individual; but it is not determined in advance which of these are satisfied by the individual; the speaker may not know exactly which ones are satisfied by that individual, and in any case his use of the name does not specify that certain of these descriptive phrases or all of them are in fact satisfied by the individual.[1]

Let us suppose that it is true that the speaker could still have referred successfully to Napoleon even if Napoleon was in fact born in 1768 instead of 1769. This does not show that the Abbreviation Theory of Referring is false, nor does it provide support for Searle's own theory of the referring use of names as against the Abbreviation Theory of Referring. For this fact can be accounted for by the Abbreviation Theory of Referring too. From what Searle says about cases in which half of the properties in question were had by one individual and the other half by a different individual, it appears that he would say that the speaker succeeds in referring to an individual only if that individual has a sufficient number of the properties mentioned in the allegedly presupposed descriptive phrases. Searle's only claim is that what these properties are is not determined in advance of the use of the name or specified by the use of the name. But what this shows at most is not that the name is not being used in one of its meanings or that names are not abbreviations of descriptions but instead that names are abbreviations of descriptions which have a certain form. It shows at most that a name is an abbreviation of one or more descriptive phrases having the form 'the individual who has a sufficient number of the properties $\emptyset, \mathcal{V}, \Theta$'. An example of such a descriptive phrase would be this: 'the individual who had a

[1] J. Searle, 'Proper Names', *Mind*, LXVII (1958) pp. 166–73. Reprinted in C. Caton (ed.), *Philosophy and Ordinary Language* (University of Illinois Press, 1963), pp. 154–61. References will be to *Mind*.

sufficient number of the properties "being a French Emperor", "being born in 1769", "being an artillery officer in the French army", and "having invaded Russia in 1812" '. If the name 'Napoleon' were an abbreviation of this descriptive phrase, then it is possible for a speaker to use the name 'Napoleon' in this meaning (the meaning of this descriptive phrase) and still succeed in referring to Napoleon even if it is not true, and moreover known to be not true, that Napoleon was born in 1769. Thus, the fact, if it is a fact, about the referring use of names on which the objection is based is not in any way incompatible with the Abbreviation Theory of Referring. The Abbreviation Theory of Referring need only say that names abbreviate descriptions, such as that exemplified above, which mention not only certain properties but also the property of possessing a sufficient number of those other properties.

It might then be objected that the set of properties which would be mentioned in such a description is open-ended and that the speaker cannot specify in advance the members of this set, as the formula 'the individual who has a sufficient number of $\emptyset$, $\mathcal{U}$, Θ' implies that he can. But it is doubtful that a speaker would be said to have referred either successfully or unsuccessfully to an individual unless he could, before or while using the name, specify some properties the possession of a sufficient number of which render an individual the individual to whom he is referring. To put this another way, the speaker must know enough about the individual to whom he is referring to make *that* individual (rather than another) the one to whom he is referring. Otherwise he is not referring to any individual or at least is not doing so intentionally. (As we will see later, a speaker can refer to an individual unintentionally.) If the speaker does not know something which picks out that individual or some one individual, then he is not referring to that individual or to any individual. And it is this set of properties—the properties which the speaker would mention before using the name if asked to specify *completely* the individual to whom he is referring—that constitutes the set of properties a sufficient number of which an individual must have to be the individual referred to.

It is, of course, possible for an individual to have a sufficient number of such properties and still not be the individual to whom the speaker succeeded in referring. For there could be another individual who also had a sufficient number of such properties. In order for an individual to be the individual to whom the speaker succeeded in referring, that individual must be the *only* individual to have a sufficient number of such properties if the name abbreviates a description of the form described above and is used in the meaning of that description.

3 *Abbreviating non-uniquely characterizing descriptions*

Searle also objects to one form of the Abbreviation Theory of Referring—the form which holds that each name is an abbreviation of a description of the following sort, 'the individual who is spatio-temporally continuous with an individual originally named "Ross" '—by saying that there may be more than one individual characterized by this description.[1] In fact this objection could be made in connection with many other sorts of descriptions, since there are many other sorts of descriptions that can characterize more than one individual at a time.

But that a description can characterize more than one individual at a time does not show that a name cannot abbreviate that description, that is, have the same meaning as that description. First, if that description is the only description abbreviated by the name and that description does characterize more than one individual at the time at which the name is used, then the speaker does not succeed in referring to a particular individual by using that name. But that the speaker does not succeed in referring to a particular individual by using a name does not show that the name is not an abbreviation of that description. After all, it is possible not to succeed in referring to an individual by using a name. And that the abbreviated description characterizes more than one individual is one reason why a speaker might not succeed in doing so in a given case. Second, while the name might abbreviate a description which characterizes more than one individual, it might also (at the same time) abbreviate another description which does uniquely characterize an individual. And if the name is used by the speaker to "stand for"[2] the latter description, then the speaker can

[1] Searle (*op. cit.*), pp. 169–70.
[2] A name is said to "stand for" a description if the name is used *in* the meaning of that description (see p. 53).

still succeed in referring to an individual by using that name.
Third, we can say, as we did in Chapter IV, that a name abbreviates
at a given time only descriptions which are uniquely characterizing
at that time.

4 *Presuppositions and the use of names*

It may be objected to the theory which I have presented that
names cannot be abbreviations of descriptions because the use of
a name does not have the same presuppositions that the use of a
descriptive phrase does. Names are held by the theory to have the
same meanings as one or more descriptive phrases. But the use of
a descriptive phrase to make a statement about an individual involves the existence of certain presuppositions. And the nature of
the presuppositions involved in using a certain type of referring
expression depends on the meaning of that expression or on the
type of meaning which it has. So, if names have the same meanings
as descriptions, the use of names should involve the same sorts of
presuppositions as does the use of descriptions. But the use of
names does not involve the same sorts of presuppositions as does
the use of descriptions. Consequently, names are not abbreviations
of descriptions.

But what is the difference between the presuppositions of the
use of names and the presuppositions of the use of descriptions?
Clark, who raises this objection to the Abbreviation Theory of
Referring, suggests the following as presuppositions of the use of
the name 'George' to make a statement about an individual:
"There is someone who is now being referred to or who is con-
ventionally referred to by the name 'George' " and "There is
someone named 'George' ".[1] Statements made by the use of, for
example, the descriptive referring phrase 'the leader of the Opposition' have the presupposition: "There is someone who is the
Leader of the Opposition". Clark says that these two types of presuppositions are very different from one another, the main difference being, according to him, that the presupposition of the use
of a name *mentions* that name while the presupposition of the use
of a description *uses* that description or part of that description.

[1] R. Clark, 'Presuppositions, Names, and Descriptions', *Philosophical Quarterly*, VI
(1956), pp. 148, 150.

This is said to show that the presupposition of the use of a name has a "linguistic character" while that of the use of a description has or carries an "existential commitment".[1] Presumably what is meant here is that the presupposition of the use of a name is at least partly about that name itself, while that of the use of a description is wholly about the world and not at all about the description itself. The objection is that since the use of names and the use of descriptive phrases have presuppositions which differ in this way, names do not stand for descriptive phrases.

But this does not seem to be correct. It seems that if it is true that names are used to abbreviate descriptions, and if, by being used *in* one meaning rather than another, a name is used to stand for one description rather than another, then the presupposition of the use of a name must mention that name and should be expected to do so. For if names are abbreviations of descriptions, then the use of the name 'Jones' would have the presupposition "Either the name 'Jones' abbreviates only one descriptive phrase or else the speaker is using the name 'Jones' in one (or perhaps more) of its several meanings". The term 'presupposition' is used, by Strawson and others, to refer to statements whose truth is a necessary condition of the speaker's having said something which is true or false by uttering certain words. For example, unless there is an individual who is Ø, according to Strawson, the speaker has not said anything that is either true or false by using the descriptive phrase 'the individual who is Ø' in the subject position of a putative statement. On this use of the term 'presupposition', it is certainly true that the above statement "Either the name 'Jones' abbreviates only one descriptive phrase or else the speaker is using the name 'Jones' in one (or perhaps more) of its several meanings" is a presupposition of any statement made by using the name 'Jones'. For on the Abbreviation Theory of Referring, unless the name 'Jones' has just one meaning or is being used in one (or perhaps more) of its several meanings, the speaker will not have referred to anyone by using the name 'Jones' and hence will not have said anything which is either true or false. This shows that if names are abbreviations of descriptions and are used to stand for descriptions, then it is to be expected that the presuppositions of their use mention those names themselves. Consequently, this ob-

[1] Clark (*op. cit.*), p. 150.

jection to the Abbreviation Theory of Referring is not sound. That the use of names and the use of descriptions differ in some presuppositions is quite compatible with this theory.

5 *Necessary truths*

Another possible objection to the Abbreviation Theory of Referring is this. On the version of this theory which I have been defending, it is clear that a name of an individual does not abbreviate the complete set of descriptions which characterize that individual. And although the name will at a given time abbreviate the complete set of descriptions which uniquely characterize that individual at that time, a given token of that name as used by a speaker will not in general *stand for* each of the descriptions in this set. It is sometimes objected[1] that if a name does abbreviate every description which characterizes a given individual, then every true statement made about that individual by the use of that name will be a necessary truth, whereas it is clear that at least many such statements are not necessary truths.

But this version of this type of objection does not apply to the theory which I am defending. For, on the theory which I am defending, a name abbreviates only uniquely characterizing descriptions. Let us suppose that Ø is a property which is not mentioned at a given time in any description which uniquely characterizes the individual in question. Then the statement "John is Ø", made at that time, is not a necessary truth if it is true at all. For Ø is not mentioned by using 'John' here, since Ø is not mentioned in any description which 'John' abbreviates. That is, the speaker is not in this case making the statement "The individual who is Ø, Θ, and so on, is Ø". The speaker is not making an analytic statement in this case.

However, it may then be objected that, given any property of an individual, there is a description which uniquely characterizes that individual and which mentions Ø. Here is the way in which this description is formed: Take any description which does uniquely characterize the individual and add mention of Ø to that description; the resulting expanded description will still uniquely characterize that individual. And then the above objection can be made

---

[1] For example, by Searle (*op. cit.*), pp. 169–70.

with respect to uniquely characterizing descriptions. We can reply to this in the following way. We can say that statements which are not necessary truths can still be made about that individual by using that name since the speaker can use that name to stand for some uniquely characterizing description which does not mention Ø, even if there is some other uniquely characterizing description which does mention Ø. Whether or not a statement is analytic, in a case in which that statement is made by using an ambiguous term, depends on what meaning that term is used in or on which description the name is used to stand for, not on the complete set of meanings which that term has.

Nevertheless, it may be said, even if a name abbreviates only some of the descriptions which characterize the individual and even if a given token of the name is used to stand for just one description, there are still some true statements about the individual made by using the name which will be necessary truths on the Abbreviation Theory of Referring which I am defending but which in fact are not necessary truths. These necessary truths will be those statements in which properties are predicated of the individual where those predicated properties are in fact mentioned by the description for which the name is allegedly used to stand. And yet certainly not all such statements, if indeed any of them, are necessary truths. For example, if the name 'Walter' is used by the speaker to stand for (that is, used in the same meaning as the meaning of) the description 'the oldest man in Room 2732 of the Empire State Building', then the statement "Walter is in Room 2732 of the Empire State Building" is, if true, a necessary truth. But this statement is, if true, certainly not a necessary truth.

In order to answer this objection, we must make it clear why the objector believes that this statement made in these circumstances is not a necessary truth. One reason for this belief might be this. The property "being in Room 2732 of the Empire State Building" is not a property which Walter necessarily has. This statement could have therefore been false since, for example, Walter could very well have been in some other room at the time at which the statement was made. This seems to be a reasonable basis on which to make this objection. But it must be noticed that if this is the foundation of the objection, then the objector is maintaining that a subject–predicate statement "X is $Ø$" is a necessary truth if and only if X necessarily has $\emptyset$. Now it is true that if 'Walter' is used to stand for the description 'the oldest man in Room 2732 of the Empire State Building', then the *sentence* 'Walter is in Room 2732 of the Empire State Building' is analytic. For this sentence has the same meaning as the sentence 'The oldest man in Room 2732 of the Empire State Building is in Room 2732 of the Empire State Building' and the latter is certainly analytic if anything is. But it is one thing for a *sentence* to be analytic and, given the objector's view of necessary truth, quite another thing for a *statement* made by using that sentence to be a necessary truth. In particular, a contingent statement may be made by using an analytic sentence, given the above view of necessary truth. Walter is here being referred to in such a way that the sentence used is analytic; but the statement made by using this sentence is contingent because it is not a necessary property of Walter that he be in Room 2732 of the Empire State Building.

Thus, this objection does not count against the Abbreviation Theory of Referring. The theory would claim that the sentence in question—'Walter is in Room 2732 of the Empire State Building' —is analytic. But it says nothing about whether or not the use of analytic sentences always results in the making of necessarily true statements. The theory is committed to no position at all on this matter. Hence, proponents of the theory can agree, consistently with their theory, that the statement in question is not a necessary truth.

The objection just discussed is raised by Wilson, who says "Suppose that the proper name 'a' means '$(\imath x)(Px)$', which in turn is equivalent to '$E!\,(\imath x)(Px)$'. The sentence 'Pa'—with 'a' defined as above—I shall call 'conditionally analytic' in the sense that the following is true: 'If there is such a thing as a then necessarily a is P' ".[1] But, according to Wilson, an individual can be the individual that he is and yet it not be necessary that that individual have a certain property in order to be that individual. Yet if names are abbreviations of descriptions, then this is necessary for each individual who has a name. For example, if the name 'a' means "the individual who is P", then if there is an individual who has the name 'a', that individual must have P. Since it is not necessary for

[1] N. L. Wilson, 'In Defense of Proper Names Against Descriptions', *Philosophical Studies*, IV (1953), p. 73.

an individual who has a certain name to have a certain property, names are not abbreviations of descriptive referring phrases.

But, as we have seen, this is not correct. If a name is an abbreviation of a descriptive phrase, then what is necessary is not that a certain individual have a certain property, but instead that a certain individual have that property *in order for* that individual to be successfully referred to by the use of that name. If a given individual does not have that property, then that individual cannot be successfully referred to by the use of that name. But it does not follow from this that if that individual does have that property and is successfully referred to by the use of that name, then that individual necessarily has that property. This individual could have not had this property, in which case that individual would have not been successfully referred to by the use of that name. It is correct to say that if '*a*' stands for a descriptive phrase which mentions property *P*, the statement "*a* is *P*" involves a conditional necessity. But this necessity does not concern the matter of that individual's being the individual that he is. Instead, it concerns that individual's being the individual whom the speaker succeeded in referring to and hence whom the statement is about. If a given individual did not have *P*, that individual would not be the individual whom the statement "*a* is *P*" is about, although that individual would still be that individual.

6 *Conveying new information to the hearer*

In the previous section we saw that the Abbreviation Theory of Referring does not imply that being in Room 2732 of the Empire State Building is a property which the individual referred to as 'Walter' necessarily has. We saw that while the speaker in this case might be using an analytic *sentence*, he was not necessarily making a *statement* which is a necessary truth.

But then a closely related objection might be made. It might be said that if the speaker does use an analytic sentence—in this case, the sentence 'The oldest man in Room 2732 of the Empire State Building is in Room 2732'—then the speaker is not conveying new information to the hearer. After all, to tell someone that the oldest man in a certain room is in that room is not to tell him anything that he did not know before. But the statement "Walter is in

Room 2732 of the Empire State Building" can be used to convey new information to a hearer. Hence this token of 'Walter' cannot stand for the description in question. And since similar cases can be given for any description at all, the name cannot abbreviate or stand for any description.

But there is information which the speaker can convey by making this statement even if he makes this statement by using an analytic sentence. If it is true that every statement made by using a descriptive phrase has presuppositions, then so does this one. This statement, even though made by using an analytic sentence, has as a presupposition (in the sense of 'presupposition' explained in Section 4 of this chapter) the statement "There is someone who is the oldest man in Room 2732 of the Empire State Building". The hearer may not have known that there is such a man. And the hearer may come to know or at least to believe this in virtue of the speaker's making his statement. The speaker may in this way give the hearer to understand that there is such a man, and thus this may be one way of conveying information to the hearer. The speaker may even have made the statement with the intention that the hearer thereby come to have this belief.

It may perhaps be replied that this information—the information conveyed by the presupposition—is different from that conveyed by the statement "Walter is in Room 2732 of the Empire State Building" and that this information is conveyed in a different way from the way the latter is conveyed. In the case of the presupposition, the information that there is *someone* who has certain properties is conveyed, while in the case of the statement made by using the name, the information that *a certain particular individual* has a certain property is conveyed. Second, the speaker conveys the former information by implying that a certain statement (the presupposition) is true, while he conveys the latter information merely through what he asserts and not by what he also implies.

We have already seen, however, in Section 4, that if the name does stand for a description, then the statement made by using the name has the presupposition that the statement made by using the descriptive phrase has. So both statements *could* convey the information embodied in the presupposed statement. And this information will be conveyed to a hearer who knows what description the name stands for. So if we can show that the statement

"Walter is in Room 2732 of the Empire State Building" can convey information that a certain particular individual has a certain property even if the name is used to stand for the description in question, we will have shown that it is possible for this statement made by using the name to convey all of the required kinds of information to the hearer even when the name is used to stand for the description in question. The type of situation which we need here is this: the hearer identifies whom the statement is about by a different descriptive phrase from that abbreviated by and stood for by the name. Let us suppose that the hearer believes that the speaker is talking about the individual whom he (the hearer) met last Wednesday. And let us further suppose that the individual whom the hearer met last Wednesday is identical with the oldest man in Room 2732 of the Empire State Building. Then the hearer is being told that a certain particular individual, whom the hearer identifies in a certain way, has a certain property. And this may well be new information for the hearer. Thus, the statement made by using the name 'Walter' to stand for a description can be used in at least some situations to convey new information to a hearer even when the property predicated of the individual referred to is a property which is mentioned in the abbreviated description. Whether or not this information is in fact conveyed to the hearer depends partly on what the hearer already knows and on the way in which he identifies the individual being talked about.

The following objection might be made to what has just been said. If we allow the speaker to succeed in conveying information to the hearer in a case in which the hearer identifies the individual in question by the use of a different description from that for which the used name stands, then we must also say that the speaker succeeds in conveying information to the hearer in the following case: the speaker uses a name and thereby succeeds in referring to a certain particular individual; but the hearer uses a description for purposes of identifying the individual being talked about where this description is not only different from the abbreviated description but also is uniquely satisfied by a different individual from that whom the speaker succeeded in referring to; as it happens, the individual whom the hearer identifies has the same property that the speaker attributed to the individual whom he was talking about; as a result of hearing what the speaker said, the hearer comes to believe that the individual whom he identified has the property in question, as indeed that individual does; so the hearer has come to believe that a true statement is true as a result of what the speaker said, even though the speaker did not make that statement. And yet this does not seem to be a case of the speaker's conveying information to the hearer.

But one who says what we said in the paragraph before the preceding one need not also say that this is a case of conveying information to the hearer. What we should say here is that the hearer's identifying the individual about whom the speaker is in fact talking as the one about whom the speaker is talking is a necessary condition of the speaker's succeeding in conveying information to the hearer in cases of this sort. But of course the hearer may satisfy this condition by using a certain description to make the identification where that description is different from that for which the used token of the proper name stands.

7 Verifying statements made by using names and descriptions

Wilson claims that names are not abbreviations for descriptions for the following reason:

> Sentences containing descriptions expand into multiple general sentences which are not decisively verifiable and are decisively falsified only under special conditions, namely, the discovery of two or more individuals satisfying the matrix of the description. . . . A singular sentence . . . is presumably both decisively verifiable and decisively falsifiable. . . . Any doubt as to the truth-value of a singular sentence does *not* arise from inability to examine all individuals.[1]

Since Wilson concludes from this that names are not abbreviations of descriptions, he must include in the class of singular statements statements which contain names and which are of the form 'Jones is P'. Presumably what Wilson means here is this. A statement of the form 'The individual that is F is also G' can be represented by the following schema: $(Ey) (Gy. (x) (Fx \equiv x=y))$. That is, such a statement asserts the existence of one and only one individual who has the property F. Therefore, ascertaining whether this statement is true involves finding out whether it is in fact true

---

[1] Wilson, (*op. cit.*), p. 73.

that there is only one such individual. And finding out that there is only one such individual involves examining all of the individuals in the universe. But the verification of statements containing proper names as their subjects does not require the examination of every individual in the universe. Consequently, names do not have the same meanings as descriptions. Hence, names are not abbreviations of descriptions.

But this is not correct. The *verification* of statements made by using names requires examination of all of the individuals in the universe just as much or just as little as the verification of statements made by using descriptive phrases does. For descriptions are involved in coming to know *about whom the speaker is talking when he uses a name*. It is possible that several individuals have that name, in which case it must be determined which of these individuals is the one being talked about. And determining this ultimately involves the use of a descriptive phrase. For example, it is determined that the speaker is referring to the individual who is P rather than the individual who is Q; but this involves finding out if there is only one individual who is P; otherwise it would not be known whether the speaker is in fact referring to this particular individual when he says that he is referring to the individual who is P; and this requires examination of all of the individuals in the universe, if it is true that examination of all of the individuals in the universe is required for the verification of statements containing descriptive phrases.

Two replies might then be made to this. First, there may in some cases be only one individual with the used name, so that descriptions do not have to be used in these cases in finding out which individuals the speaker is talking about. Second, when the speaker answers the question "Whom are you talking about?", he may reply by giving another name of that individual instead of giving a description which that individual satisfies, and there may be only one individual who has both of these names. Both of these replies cite the possibility of there being only one individual with a certain name. But what we are dealing with here is the verifying of statements and consequently with people coming to have knowledge. So even if it is the case that only one individual *does* have a certain name, nevertheless, someone can *find out* that only one individual has this name only if he examines all of the individuals in the universe. And he must find this out if he is to verify the statement in question. For in order to verify the statement in question, he must know whom it is that the speaker is talking about by using that name. If the person performing the verification has only a name to go on, then he must find out if more than one individual has that name. For if more than one individual has that name, the name by itself is not sufficient to tell him who it is that the speaker's statement is about. So the verification of statements made by the use of names seems to require examination of all individuals in the universe to the same extent as the verification of statements made by the use of descriptions does.

Wilson seems to believe that it is already known whom a statement made by using a name is about before the process of verification of the statement begins, and that then the process of verification consists only in examining that individual to see if that individual has the property in question. But in fact before the process of verification of such statements can take place, it must be determined which individual it is that the statement is about. And determining this may involve the examination of all of the individuals in the universe, just as it may in the case of the use of a description. Of course, it is possible that it may already be known that only one individual in the universe has the name in question or that one can come to know this without examining all of the individuals in the universe. But in whatever way this can be known, it is also possible to know in this way that there is only one individual who satisfies a certain descriptive phrase. So statements made by the use of names do not differ in this way from statements made by the use of descriptive phrases.

8 Names and spatio-temporal locations of individuals

Now I wish to discuss two particular theories which are versions of the Abbreviation Theory of Referring. Each of these theories makes a claim about what type of descriptions it is that names abbreviate. I have said that a name may abbreviate descriptions of many different types, while each of these theories claims that there is one and only one type of description which a name abbreviates or even can abbreviate. Thus, these theories are incompatible with what I have said earlier, and constitute objections to what I have said. I will try to show that each of these two theories is incorrect.

Zink says:

> Thus the meaning of a particular proper name 'P.N.' would be the meaning of the expression 'the person truly named "P.N." who is or was at the time T at place P'.[1]

Zink also says that if there are several persons named 'P.N.', the name 'P.N.' will have more than one meaning.[2] But he holds that each meaning of a proper name involves mention of a spatio-temporal location of the individual in question and that no other type of description can have the same meaning as a proper name. His reason for saying this seems to be that such descriptions—those mentioning spatio-temporal locations—are "adequate to identifying the person".[3] But one may know who many persons are without knowing anything about their location at the present or at any previous moment. Zink's reply is that these descriptions embody knowledge about the individual but not about the meaning of that individual's name. He further claims that other types of descriptions enable us to "locate" individuals because these descriptions "entail" descriptions which involve mention of locations. For example, he claims that the description 'thirty-fourth President of the United States of America' entails the description 'is located in Washington, D.C., at some times within a certain time span'.[4]

But this position does not seem to be correct. It seems that the only reason why someone might maintain this position is that he believes that if a proper name has a meaning, that name has *that* meaning at *every* moment after it comes to have that meaning. And he may believe that the only property which an individual must continue to have is the property of having been at a certain place at a certain time, and hence that the meaning of that name must mention that and only that sort of property. But this is not true. If an individual was the first person to build an aeroplane, then that person has that property of being the first person to have built an aeroplane at every moment after the moment at which he comes to have this property. And the description 'the first person

---

[1] S. Zink, 'The Meaning of Proper Names', *Mind*, LXXII (1963), p. 491.
[2] *Ibid.*, p. 492.   [3] *Ibid.*, p. 491.   [4] *Ibid.*, p. 495.

to have built an aeroplane' not only does not mention a spatio-temporal location but also does not "entail" a description which does mention such a location.

Zink talks about "locating" individuals. It is clear that the speaker need not "locate" an individual for a hearer in the sense of directly providing that hearer with information about the individual's spatio-temporal location in order to have either referred successfully to that individual or identified that individual for the hearer. And this would be so even if it were true that hearers were necessarily involved in successful referring. After all, a speaker can refer successfully to an individual by using the description 'the first person to have built an aeroplane'. It would perhaps be replied that while it may be true that a speaker can refer successfully to an individual by using this non-spatio-temporal description, he cannot do so by using a name which has the same meaning as this non-spatio-temporal description. And even if the speaker did use the name to stand for that description, he would not be using that name in one of its meanings, for that description does not and cannot have the same meaning as that name. But if this description can be used to refer successfully to an individual, why can't a name be used in the meaning of this description to do so too? Someone may say that when the individual was given that name, he did not have the property of being the first person to have built an aeroplane. So the meaning of that name could not have mentioned this property at that time; and therefore the meaning of that name could not mention this property at a later time too. This does not show that Zink's position is correct, however. First, it is not necessarily the case that at the time at which that individual was given that name, the only property which that individual and only that individual had was the property of being in a certain location. He might have been the only one to have some other property too, in which case there seems to be no reason, on this position, why that property could not be mentioned when the meaning of that name is set out. Second, we have said in Chapter IV that a name can have a different meaning at each different moment. Hence, even if at a certain time the meaning of a name involves the location of the individual who was given that name, that name may have a different meaning at a later time. The name may, at that later time, be synonymous with a description which does not mention (or "entail") anything about spatio-temporal locations and yet uniquely characterizes that individual at that later time. The name may have the same meaning as that description does at that later time.

Zink says "The meaning of a word is that which enables us to use it".[1] But there is nothing in the nature of a spatio-temporal description which would allow it to enable a name to be used which could not also be true of a non-spatio-temporal description. Each type may not only uniquely characterize an individual but also uniquely characterize that individual as long as that individual has that name. Hence, we may say that names can have the same meanings as non-spatio-temporal descriptions.

9 *Indexical descriptive phrases*

Burks claims that proper names are synonymous with indexical descriptions.[2] An indexical definite description has the form 'this P' or contains a part which has this form. An example of the type of description which, on Burks's view, is synonymous with a name is: "the man who is P in this room". He seems to hold that different tokens of the same name can be abbreviations for different descriptions.[3]

A proponent of this position could be maintaining either one or both of the following theses: (I) a proper name necessarily has the same meaning as one or more indexical descriptions and only these indexical descriptions; (II) a proper name as a matter of contingent fact has the same meaning as one or more indexical descriptions and only these descriptions, though it could have or

---

[1] Zink (*op. cit.*), p. 490.

[2] A. Burks, 'A Theory of Proper Names', *Philosophical Studies*, II (1951), pp. 37, 38, 43.

[3] Burks also says that given a type-name, such as 'John', all tokens of this type either have the same "designatum" or else fail to have any "designatum" (p. 43). This seems to be false. According to Burks, it is tokens, not types, that have what he calls "designata". He does not explain what he means by the term 'designatum', but presumably since it is tokens that have designata and tokens of names are used to refer to particular individuals, the designatum of a given token is the individual to whom that token is used to refer. But then different tokens of the same type-name can have different designata because these tokens can be used to refer to different individuals. One speaker might use one such token to refer to one individual while another speaker might use another such token to refer to another individual.

have had instead or in addition the same meaning as one or more non-indexical descriptions. (11) may be true. But Burks's arguments do not and could not give (11) any support. His arguments seem intended to support (1) instead. But they also do not give (1) any support.

What are the arguments for the view that a proper name is an abbreviation of an indexical descriptive phrase? The first argument which Burks gives is not intended to show that names abbreviate indexical descriptions. Instead it is intended to show that *if* names do abbreviate indexical descriptions, those descriptions cannot be wholly indexical. That is, such descriptions must contain a non-indexical element if they contain an indexical element. Burks says that this is because an indexical term or phrase, such as the term 'this', is "existentially related" to many objects and therefore does not by itself indicate just one of those objects rather than another.[1] Consequently, the abbreviated description must contain a general term or phrase, as well as an indexical element, in order that the name may indicate which of the objects to which the indexical element is "existentially related" is being referred to by the use of that name.

But, given that a name stands for or in some way abbreviates a descriptive phrase, what reason is there to believe that that descriptive phrase contains any indexical element at all? Burks's argument for this seems to be as follows. He tries to show that the statement "Truman plays the piano" made by using the name 'Truman' is not synonymous with, for example, the statement "The x that has T plays the piano", where 'T' stands for some non-indexical property that is had by Truman. It is possible that the universe be such that two x's have T, in which case the first statement would be true while the second statement is false, since the second statement asserts, according to Burks, that there is one and only one individual who is T. Since a situation in which these two statements can have different truth-values is thus possible, these two statements are not synonymous with one another.[2] But these two statements differ from one another only with respect to the referring phrases which they contain. Consequently, these referring phrases—'Truman' and 'the x that is T'—cannot be synonymous with one another. Hence, this token of 'Truman' is

[1] Burks (*op. cit.*), p. 41.   [2] *Ibid.*, p. 42.

79

not an abbreviation for 'the x that is T'. Therefore, if 'Truman' abbreviates any descriptive phrase at all, it must abbreviate one which contains something other than a purely descriptive element. The only other kind of element that a descriptive phrase can contain is an indexical element. Hence, if 'Truman' is an abbreviation of a descriptive phrase at all, it must be an abbreviation of an indexical description, such as 'this x that is T'. An expression of this sort will apply to only one individual even in a universe in which there is more than one individual who has T.

It is assumed in the above argument that when a descriptive phrase of the form 'the x that is T' is used to refer to an individual, the speaker thereby asserts that there is one and only one individual who is T. It is for this reason that the second of the two statements cited above is regarded by Burks as false in the above situation. It does not, however, seem to me to be true that the speaker is asserting this. Instead, it seems to be the case that the speaker is presupposing this in the sense of 'presupposition' described in Section 4 of this chapter. But even if this is presupposed rather than asserted, an argument very similar to Burks's argument can be given. It is this. Suppose that there are two x's who are T, just as in the above situation. Since this is the same situation as that described by Burks, Burks would say that in this situation the statement "Truman plays the piano" is true. But the presupposition of the utterance "The x that is T plays the piano" is not true. Since this presupposition is not true, the speaker has not succeeded in making a statement—that is, in saying something which is either true or false—by uttering this sentence. Hence, the speaker says something which is true by using the name 'Truman' but does not do so by using the description 'the x that is T'. Consequently, this token of 'Truman' cannot have the same meaning as this description.

Let us consider (11) first. Does this argument support (11)? (11) is the empirical claim that as a matter of fact names abbreviate indexical descriptions and only such descriptions. This argument does not support (11). The described situation is one in which, *if* it is the case that 'Truman' abbreviates the given non-indexical description, the speaker will not succeed in making a statement about an individual, since he cannot do so by using the non-indexical description itself. What this shows is that *if* the speaker does succeed in making a statement about an individual in this situation by using the name 'Truman', then that name does not abbreviate a non-indexical description. But to show this is not to show that the name does not abbreviate a non-indexical description. It only shows that *if* a certain condition is fulfilled, then the name does not abbreviate a non-indexical description. It shows at most that if a certain condition is fulfilled, then if the name abbreviates a description at all, the name abbreviates an indexical description. But, it may be said, this condition—namely, that the speaker succeed in referring to, and in making a statement which is about, a particular individual—can be fulfilled in this situation. But this does not show that the name *does* abbreviate an indexical description. It only shows that the name *can* abbreviate an indexical description. It shows only that in this situation a name must abbreviate an indexical description *if* the speaker is to succeed in referring to a particular individual and in making a statement that is either true or false by using that name. But this does not show (*a*) that in every situation the speaker will succeed in referring to an individual by using a name, and hence does not show that in every situation any name which the speaker uses does abbreviate an indexical description. Nor does this show (*b*) that in other types of situations—for example, in situations in which there is one and only one individual who is *T*—names abbreviate indexical descriptions and only indexical descriptions. Consequently, this argument does not show that all names in fact do abbreviate indexical descriptions and only such descriptions. It follows from this that this argument does not support (1) either. For if this argument does not show that names *do* abbreviate only such descriptions, this argument does not show that names *must* abbreviate only such descriptions.

It is quite compatible with this argument that a given token is used to stand for a non-indexical description—for example, 'the *x* that is *T*'. Of course, if there are two *x*'s that are *T*, then the speaker, in using the token to stand for a non-indexical description, will not succeed in referring to an individual. But there is no guarantee that in using a certain name—especially a name such as 'Truman', which is a name of more than one individual—the speaker will always succeed in referring to an individual or in saying something that is either true or false. It is true that there are possible situations in which a speaker will succeed in referring to an individual only if he uses a token of a name as standing for an indexical description. But it is compatible with this that not all tokens of names are used to stand for indexical descriptions. For it is compatible with this that there be situations in which the speaker does not succeed in referring to an individual. And it is furthermore compatible with this that if a name is not used to stand for an indexical description but is instead used to stand for a wholly non-indexical description, the speaker may still succeed in referring to an individual and in saying something true or false about that individual by the use of that token. For the situation may be one in which only one individual has property T.

Burks also says that if a speaker did use a token to abbreviate a non-indexical description, the speaker could not know that he had succeeded in referring to an individual or to the individual to whom he intended to refer.[1] But it is possible that there are cases in which the speaker does not know this. Some of these cases are cases in which he does succeed in referring to that individual while others are not such cases. And it is also possible that there are cases in which the speaker can know that he has succeeded in referring to an individual even if he uses the token to stand for a non-indexical description. For the speaker may believe truly on good grounds that there is only one individual who is characterized by that non-indexical description.

[1] Burks (*op. cit.*), p. 42.

VI

THE INTENTION–DESCRIPTION
THEORY OF REFERRING

I

1 *Introduction*

In the preceding two chapters I described and defended a version of the Abbreviation Theory of Referring. One of the fundamental and essential doctrines of this version of the theory is that a speaker can use a token of a name *in* one of the meanings of that name. To put this in another way, a speaker can use the token to *stand for* one of the descriptive referring phrases with which that name is synonymous. But what does the speaker do when he uses a token of a name *in* one of its meanings or to *stand for* one description? What I say in this chapter and the next can be construed as having either one of two purposes. The theory described and defended here can be regarded as complementary to the version of the Abbreviation Theory of Referring presented in the preceding chapters—in fact as part of that theory and as an essential addition to that theory. For the theory presented in this chapter—which I call "The Intention–Description Theory of Referring"—can be regarded as constituting an answer to the above question: What is the speaker doing when he uses a token of a name *in* one of its meanings or to *stand for* one description? But the Intention–Description Theory of Referring can be regarded in another way too. This theory provides a solution to the problem of ambiguous reference described in Chapter I (to which the Abbreviation Theory of Referring also provides a solution). And the Intention–Description Theory of Referring gives such a solution without any mention of meanings and without asserting that names have meanings. This theory gives what might be called a "descriptivist" solution to this problem, just as the Abbreviation Theory of Referring does. For both theories assert that when the speaker succeeds in referring to a particular individual[1] by using a name or descriptive phrase which applies to more than one individual, the speaker succeeds in doing so in virtue of the existence of a certain relation between the used (that is, uttered) token of the name or description on the one hand and another descriptive referring phrase on the other.[2] According to the Abbreviation Theory of Referring, the relation in question is that of abbreviation in the sense of the term 'abbreviation' described in Section 1 of Chapter IV: if the used token is a token of a name, then that token is synonymous with the descriptive referring phrase in question; if the used token is a token of a descriptive referring phrase, then the used token is part of the abbreviated descriptive referring phrase (in the way in which, for example, the description 'the Senator' is part of the description 'the senior Senator from New York'). This relation might also be called the relation of "standing for": the name token stands for the description with which the token is synonymous, as was said in Chapter V; and the description token stands for the larger or more complete description of which this token is a part. As we have also seen, this raises the question: What is it for a name token to be synonymous with just one description and what makes the token synonymous with that description rather than with some other description; and what is it for a description token to stand for just one of the descriptions of which it is a part, and what makes the description token stand for that description rather than for another description of which it is also a part? It was said that the Intention–Description Theory of Referring provides answers to these questions. And so the Intention–Description

[1] It may be well to remind the reader at this point that when I say that a speaker is trying to refer to, or succeeds in referring to, a particular individual, I am using the word 'particular' in such a way that I mean that he is trying to refer to, or succeeds in referring to, *a certain individual*, not to just any one individual of a certain type. *I mean that he is referring or trying to refer to a particular one of these individuals*.

[2] An example of a 'non-descriptivist' theory of referring would be one in which names pick out individuals in some ostensive way, as pointing does—in any case, one in which names pick out individuals without necessarily having any relation to a description.

Theory of Referring can be regarded as a part of the Abbreviation Theory of Referring. But the answers to these questions which are given by the Intention–Description Theory of Referring can be given without mentioning the meaning of name-tokens and without mentioning the fact that a description–token is part of another description. That is, the relation, mentioned previously, between the used tokens and the descriptive referring phrases can be described by the Intention–Description Theory of Referring without mentioning the relation of synonymy or the part–whole relation. So the Intention–Description Theory of Referring can be regarded as a different and alternative theory of referring. This will be shown in Section 6 of this chapter, where the relation between these two theories will be discussed further.

2 *Intending to refer to a particular individual is not a sufficient condition of succeeding in referring to that individual*

Let us suppose that a speaker utters the sentence 'Truman is tall' with the intention of referring to—that is, making a statement which is about—the present President of the United States. The speaker may, for example, mistakenly believe that the name of the present President of the United States is 'Truman' and intend to refer to (make a statement about) the present President of the United States. In this case the speaker does not succeed in referring to the individual to whom he is trying to refer. He does not succeed in making a statement which is about that individual. That the speaker intends to refer to the present President of the United States in uttering this sentence is not a sufficient condition of his succeeding in referring to the present President in this case. This speaker does not succeed in referring to the individual in question because he uses a name which is not a name of that individual. 'Truman' is not a name of the present President of the United States. Instead, let us suppose, John F. Kennedy is the present President.

That the speaker does not succeed in referring to John F. Kennedy and does not succeed in making a statement which is about John F. Kennedy can be shown in the following way. In any case in which a speaker uses a referring expression, the hearer can ask the speaker whom he is referring to, or about whom he is trying to make a statement, or whom it is that his statement is about. Let us suppose that Jones is the speaker, that Smith is the hearer, and that Jones says what he says with the intention of making a statement which is about the present President of the United States. Let us further suppose that Jones believes that both 'Truman' and 'John F. Kennedy' are names of the current President of the United States. There are at least four possible cases here:

(i) J Truman is tall.
    S Do you mean that John F. Kennedy is tall?
    J That's what I mean.

(ii) J Truman is tall.
    S Do you mean that John F. Kennedy is tall?
    J That's what I said.

(iii) J Kennedy is tall.
    S Do you mean that the current President of the United States is tall?
    J That's what I said.

(iv) J Truman is tall.
    S Do you mean that the current President of the United States is tall?
    J That's what I said.

Let us call what Jones says in the third line of each of these cases "Jones's reply." In case (i), Jones's reply is true. In case (i) Jones did "mean" John F. Kennedy. Jones is truly saying that he meant to refer to John F. Kennedy. Jones's reply in case (iii) is also true. Jones did make a statement in case (iii) which is in fact about John F. Kennedy, given that Jones's intention in uttering this sentence 'Kennedy is tall' is to make a statement which is about the current President of the United States.[1] If John F. Kennedy is not tall, then what Jones said is false. Thus, Jones's reply in case (iii) is true.

But Jones's replies in cases (ii) and (iv) are false. In case (ii) Jones did not *say* that John F. Kennedy is tall, although that is what he meant (as in case (i)). And in case (iv) Jones meant to say,

[1] We are assuming that John F. Kennedy is the current President.

86

THE INTENTION-DESCRIPTION THEORY OF REFERRING

but in fact did not say, that the current President of the United States is tall. *In cases* (11) *and* (1v), *Smith can truly say to Jones "That may be what you meant, but it is not what you said"*. That Smith can truly say this to Jones shows that in these two cases, Jones did not succeed in making a statement which is about John F. Kennedy.

These cases are concerned with statements, not sentences. It is true that in, for example, case (111) there is a sense of 'said' in which Jones did not say what he says that he said. For Jones did not utter the *sentence* which Smith used in asking his question. Jones did not utter the sentence 'The current President of the United States is tall'. But Jones' reply in this case is nevertheless true. It is true that that is what Jones said. So "what it is that Jones said" cannot be a sentence. "What it is that Jones said", about which Jones replies truly that he said that, is a *statement*. What Smith is asking about is what statement Jones was making. And that Smith uses a different sentence from that used by Jones to ask this shows that what Smith is asking is not what sentence Jones uttered—Smith already knows what sentence Jones used and that it is different from the sentence used by Smith—but instead what statement Jones was making by uttering the sentence that he (Jones) uttered. I am here using the term 'statement' in the sense explained in Section 1 of Chapter IV. That is, I am using 'statement' in the sense in which if two speakers predicate the same property of the same individual, they have made the same statement, even if they refer to that one individual by the use of two different referring expressions. What Smith is doing in these cases is asking Jones what statement it is that Jones was trying to make. For Smith uses a different sentence from that used by Jones and thereby indicates to Jones that he is not asking what words Jones used. Instead he is asking what individual Jones was trying to make a statement about and hence what statement he was trying to make. When Jones replies "That's what I said", he is saying "That's the statement that I made". The term 'said' here is being used in its sense of "statement-making".

In cases (11) and (1v) Jones's replies are false. That is, what he claims to have said is not what he did say in these cases but only what he meant to say. Since Jones used words in saying what he said which are different from the words used by Smith in asking his question about what Jones said, the term 'said' is being used in these cases in the statement-making sense, as the preceding paragraph shows. Thus, when Jones says "That's what I said", Jones is saying, "That's the statement which I made". Jones is saying that he made the *statement* about which Smith is asking his question. But since Jones's reply "That's what I said" is false in these cases, it is not true that Jones made the statement about which the hearer, Smith, is asking. But the statement about which Smith is asking differs from that which Jones was trying to make only with respect to the individual in question. The statement about which Smith is asking is about a certain individual, and this statement predicates a certain property of that individual. Jones is trying to predicate that *same* property of an individual. So these two statements do not differ with respect to the *property* being predicated. Consequently, Jones did not fail to make the statement about which Smith is asking because he predicated a different property of an individual; for he predicated (or tried to predicate) the same property of an individual. So it must be that the reason why Jones did not succeed in making the statement about which Smith is asking is this: what Jones did say was not about the individual whom the statement about which Smith is asking is about. That is, Jones did not succeed in referring to that individual. But the reason why Jones did not succeed in referring to that individual is that Jones did not use a referring expression which applies to that individual. In particular, Jones used a name which is not a name of the individual to whom he was trying to refer.

That this is the reason why Jones did not succeed in referring to the individual in question can be shown in the following way. The only difference between cases (11) and (111) with respect to what Jones says is that in (111) Jones used a name which is a name of John F. Kennedy while in (11) Jones used a name which is not a name of John F. Kennedy. And Jones did succeed in referring to the individual in question in (111), since his reply in (111) is true, while in (11) Jones did not succeed in referring to the individual in question since his reply in (11) is false. Therefore the reason why Jones did not succeed in referring to the individual in question in (11) is that Jones did not use a name of that individual. *Consequently, if a speaker uses a name to refer to an individual, then a necessary condition of his succeeding in referring to that individual is that the used name be a name of that individual.* Therefore, if a speaker uses a name to refer to an individual, it is not a sufficient condition of his succeeding in referring to that individual merely that he use that name with the intention of referring to that particular individual.

Since cases which differ from cases (i)–(iv) only in that Jones uses descriptive referring phrases rather than names can be set forth, the above argument also shows the following: *if a speaker uses a description to refer to an individual, a necessary condition of his succeeding in thereby referring to that individual is that that individual satisfy the used description.*

It follows from this that if a speaker uses a name or a description to refer to an individual, then it is not a sufficient condition of his succeeding in doing so that the speaker use that name or description with the intention of referring to or making a statement which is about that individual.

It should be pointed out that the theses just stated and argued for apply also to referring expressions when used for purposes other than the making of statements. For example, if a speaker asked a hearer "What is the best route to Chicago?" at time t_1 and later at time t_2 said "I meant New York instead of Chicago", we would not regard the speaker as having asked a question about New York at time t_1. The speaker would not have asked the question which he perhaps intended to ask, because he tried to refer to a city by using a name which is in fact not a name of that city.

At this point a possible exception to the principles defended above must be discussed. We must distinguish between a name *of* an individual and a term which is not a name of an individual but is instead someone's name *for* that individual. For example, a certain individual might have the name 'Albert' and the term 'Mac' might be someone's name for that individual. That is, the person regularly calls that individual 'Mac'; the person's calling that individual 'Mac' does not make 'Mac' a name of that individual but it does make 'Mac' that person's name for that individual. The possible exception, then, to the above principles is this: if a term 'Ø' is a person's name *for* a particular individual, then that person can make a statement which is about that individual by using the term 'Ø' even though 'Ø' is not that individual's name. Thus, for example, the person previously mentioned can make a statement about the individual in question by saying "Mac has been elected to the City Council". Moreover, a second person can make a statement about that same individual by using the term 'Mac' in certain circumstances, even if the term 'Mac' is not that second person's name for the individual. For example, let us suppose that the first person and the second person are talking with one another. The first person makes a statement about that individual by using the term 'Mac'. The second person may now use the term 'Mac' to make a statement about that same individual.

The case for this being an exception to the above principles is quite plausible. If we wanted to rule this out and not allow it to be an exception, we would have to say the following. In fact the first person does not make a statement about that individual by using the term 'Mac'. We will see later that it is possible for a speaker to convey information about an individual to a hearer by making what seems to be a statement about that individual which is in fact not a statement about that individual. And this seems to be what happens in the case of the use of a term which is someone's name for an individual. The hearers know whom the speaker is talking about, in one sense of the expression 'talking about some-one' which will be discussed in Section 10 of this chapter, even though in fact the speaker has not made a statement about that individual. Suppose that someone's name for W. H. Auden is 'George'. That person says "George is very knowledgeable about opera" with the intention of thereby making a statement about W. H. Auden. If the hearer asks the speaker "Do you mean that W. H. Auden is very knowledgeable about opera?" it seems that the speaker can truly say "That's what I said", if at all, only in special circumstances, such as its having been accepted that W. H. Auden may be referred to by use of the term 'George'. This tends to show that it is only in special circumstances, if at all, that the speaker can use 'George' to make a statement about W. H. Auden even if 'George' is that speaker's name for W. H. Auden. And it may even be the case that what these special circumstances do is allow the hearer to know whom it is that the speaker is talking about (in one sense of 'talking about someone') rather than make what the speaker says a statement which is in fact about W. H. Auden.

Whatever should be said about the above case, I think that we must regard the following case as one in which what the speaker says is *not* about the individual in question: a speaker uses the name 'Balzac' to make statements about Honoré de Balzac; but in the course of making these statements and without the topic of discussion having previously been changed, he inadvertently uses the term 'Stendhal'; for example, in the course of recounting events in Balzac's life, the speaker might inadvertently say "Stendhal made his first trip to Italy ostensibly to perform some services for the Count Guidoboni-Visconti". Here it might be said that the speaker has made a statement about Balzac in these circumstances even though he used the name 'Stendhal' in doing so, and that the speaker has done so shows that the principle being defended in this section is incorrect. But it seems that all that happens here is that the hearers know from the previous statements whom the speaker is trying to make a statement about, and that the speaker does not succeed in making a statement about that individual by using 'Stendhal'. It does seem that in this case too, if the speaker claimed to have said that Balzac made such a trip to Italy, the hearer would be justified in denying that the speaker had said that, although the hearer would say that he knew that that is what the speaker *meant* at that point. And that it is false that that is what the speaker *said* shows that the speaker did not, even in this case, make a statement about Balzac by using the term 'Stendhal'.

The term 'statement' is thus being linked with the use of the term 'said', particularly in the expression "That's what I said". 'Statement' refers to what the speaker said in this sense of 'said'. 'Statement' is not being linked with ordinary uses of the term 'refer' since, as we shall see in Section 10 of this chapter, 'refer' is ordinarily used in at least two different ways.

I have tried to show that it is not sufficient for a speaker to make a statement which is about a certain particular individual that the speaker say something with the intention of making such a statement. This is also true for statements which are not about particular individuals. For example, if a speaker utters the sentence 'Snow is white' with the intention of thereby making the statement that sugar is sweet, he does not succeed in making that statement. A more usual example is this: the speaker is learning to speak German and utters the sentence 'Schnee ist weiss' with the intention of thereby making the statement that sugar is sweet—which, of course, he does not succeed in doing. It is also necessary in these cases that the speaker utter a sentence having the appropriate meaning. And the analogue to this in the case of statements about particular individuals is, as we have seen, that the speaker use a name or a description which applies to the individual about whom the speaker is trying to make a statement.

Smith's question in cases (III) and (IV) is expressed by the use of a descriptive phrase—'the current President of the United States'—which is satisfied by one and only one individual. If such a phrase had not been used—if, that is, a descriptive phrase which applied to more than one individual had been used—then it would not be clear which statement Smith was asking about in asking his question. It could be a statement about one of the individuals who satisfied the description, or it could be a different statement, that is, a statement about another of the individuals who satisfied that description. Since Smith's question is expressed in terms of a description which uniquely characterizes an individual, the statement about which Smith is asking is thereby completely specified. *A referring expression's applying to one and only one individual is a sufficient condition of the statement made by using that expression being about that and only that individual. For the hearer can truly say to the speaker "That's what you said" with reference to that individual, regardless of what the speaker claims that he meant in such a case.*

If it is necessary in order to refer successfully to an individual by using a name or a description that the name or description apply to that individual, then this is so on any theory of referring and must be maintained by all such theories, including the Abbreviation Theory of Referring. For the argument that was given for this was not based on, and did not presuppose, any particular theory of referring.

3 *Intending to refer to a particular individual is a necessary condition of succeeding in referring to that individual in certain cases*

What was said in the preceding section shows that the speaker's intending to refer to a certain individual is not a sufficient condition of his succeeding in referring to that individual. We have seen that it is also necessary that the name or description used to make the statement apply to the individual to whom the speaker is trying to refer. That is, it is necessary that the name or description be had by or satisfied by that individual. *But I claim that in those cases in which the name or description does apply to that individual and to other individuals as well, the speaker's using that name or description with the intention of making a statement about that individual is a sufficient condition of his succeeding in referring to that individual. His using the name or description with such an intention is also a necessary condition of his succeeding in referring to that individual in such cases.* This is the answer which the Intention–Description Theory of Referring gives to the question asked in Chapter I. In cases in which the referring expression applies to more than one individual, what renders the speaker's statement a statement about one of these individuals rather than another is the speaker's intending what he says to be a statement about that individual.

This is not to say, however, that a speaker's using an expression with the intention of thereby referring to a particular individual is a necessary condition of the speaker's having thereby made a statement about that individual. For, as was just noted in the previous section, if a speaker uses a name or description which applies to *only one* individual, then the speaker's statement is about that individual regardless of whom the speaker intended to refer to. If the speaker uses the name 'J. William Fulbright' with the intention of referring to the current Secretary of State, and if the Secretary of State does not have that name, the speaker will not succeed in referring to the current Secretary of State; but if, as seems likely, there is only one individual having the name 'J. William Fulbright', then the speaker's statement is about that one individual (that is, about the current Chairman of the Senate Foreign Relations Committee). For if the speaker who utters the sentence 'J. William Fulbright is a Republican' is asked whether he meant that the current Chairman of the Senate Foreign Relations Committee is a Republican and denies it on the ground that he meant to talk about Dean Rusk (the current Secretary of State), the hearer can truly say "But that's what you said", meaning that the speaker did say that the current Chairman of that committee is a Republican, even if that is not what the speaker meant to say.

Since the speaker's statement is about the current Chairman of that committee even though the speaker intended to make a statement about a different individual, it is not necessary that the speaker intend to refer to a certain individual in order for his statement to be about that individual. But it is necessary that he intend to refer to that individual in order for his statement to be about that individual if the referring expression used by the speaker applies to more than one individual.

Thus, in order for the speaker to make a statement about a particular individual by using a name or description, it is necessary that the used name or description apply to that individual. It is also necessary that *either* the used (that is, uttered) name or description apply *only* to that individual *or* the speaker use that name or description with the *intention* of referring to that individual. *These two necessary conditions together constitute a sufficient condition of the speaker's having referred to a particular individual* (in the sense of having made a statement, if what the speaker is doing is making a statement, which is about that particular individual). If both parts of the second necessary condition are fulfilled simultaneously but in conflicting ways—as when the name or description applies to only one individual but the speaker used that name or description with the intention of referring to another individual—then the speaker's statement is about the one and only individual who has that name or satisfies that description rather than about the individual to whom the speaker intended to refer.

4 *The speaker's intention description*

I have said that in order to succeed in referring to a particular individual by using a name or description which applies to more than one individual, the speaker must have an intention of a certain sort. This intention is expressible by the speaker's making a statement of the following form: "In using '∅', I intend to refer to ——," where '∅' is the used (uttered) name or description. It is clear that the blank in this form can be filled by a description. For example, the speaker may express his intention by making the statement "In using the name 'Gluck', I intend to refer to the composer of the earliest full-length opera still regularly performed". A description which fills this position in an expression of this sort of intention will be called "the speaker's intention description" or "the intention description".

It will perhaps be said that a name can fill this position in an expression of such an intention. For example, it may be said that the speaker's intention could be expressed by the following statement in a certain case: "In using the expression 'the discoverer of Victoria Falls', I intend to refer to David Livingstone". And it is true that a name can occur in this position. But we can still talk about the speaker's intention description in a case in which a name rather than a description occupies this position in the statement that the speaker makes to express his intention. For in expressing his intention in this way, the speaker is saying either that he is trying to refer to the one and only individual named 'David Livingstone' or that he is trying to refer to one of the individuals named 'David Livingstone'.

Let us suppose that the speaker is trying to refer to the one and only individual named 'David Livingstone'. He can express his intention in this case by saying that he intends to refer to David Livingstone. But this same intention can be also expressed by the statement "In using '∅', I intend to refer to the one and only individual named 'David Livingstone'". That is, this same intention can be expressed by either using the name 'David Livingstone' or by mentioning that name as part of a descriptive phrase of the form 'the one and only individual named "∅"'. And so in this kind of case, the description 'the one and only individual named "∅"' can be regarded as the speaker's intention description. As said above, the other type of intention which the speaker could be expressing is the intention to refer to one of the individuals named 'David Livingstone'. But how will the speaker know whether or not he has carried out this intention? If there is more than one individual named 'David Livingstone', the speaker will have carried out this intention only if he has referred to just one of those individuals. But nothing in his intention picks out just one of those individuals. There is no way for the speaker to decide just which one of these individuals his statement is about, merely on the basis of his intention. Hence this is not an intention which can render the speaker's statement a statement about just one of these individuals rather than another. So it is still true that there is an intention description—a description of the form 'the ——'—

in the case of every intention which can render the speaker's statement a statement about just one particular individual.

Of course, the speaker could express his intention by saying "In using 'Ø' I intend to refer to David Livingstone" and not mean by this that he intends to refer to the one and only individual named 'David Livingstone', and yet still claim that he knows what would count as the carrying out of this intention. But he can know in this case what would count as the successful carrying out of his intention only if he has some way of picking out one particular individual. And if he has some way of picking out just one individual, that way must be cited by him in any *complete* expression of his intention. For example, the speaker may say that he will have carried out his intention if his statement is about the discoverer of Victoria Falls. But then it is the case that what the speaker intends is to refer to an individual named 'David Livingstone' who is the discoverer of Victoria Falls. And so a *complete* expression of his intention does contain an intention description— in this case, the description 'the individual named "David Livingstone" who is the discoverer of Victoria Falls'.

It might be objected that this is only because what is *meant* by a "complete" expression of intention is one which does contain such a description. But this is not so. What is meant by a complete expression of intention is a statement on the basis of which it can be determined whether or not the speaker has carried out his intention. When the speaker expresses his intention by saying "In using 'Ø', I intend to refer to David Livingstone", he uses the name 'David Livingstone' to refer to an individual. So we know what his intention is—that is, what intention he is expressing— only if we know to whom he is referring in expressing this intention in this way. He must be able to identify the individual to whom he is referring. There are only two ways of doing this. He can do this with a description, in which case his intention is completely expressed only if this description is used in doing so, as above. He can also do this by using another name, say, 'Jones'. But then he is trying to refer to the one and only individual named both 'David Livingstone' and 'Jones'. His intention description is 'the one and only individual named "David Livingstone" and "Jones" '. If there are two individuals having these two names, he will still not know which of them he is trying to refer to. But at least his intention (which now contains an intention description) will be of the sort that would enable him to know in other situations which individual he was referring to, namely situations in which there was only one individual having these two names. So it is a necessary condition of the speaker's knowing to whom he is trying to refer that his intention be expressible by the use of a description.[1] And only intentions which are such as to enable the speaker to know to whom he is trying to refer can serve the function of rendering the speaker's statement a statement about a certain individual or a particular individual in cases in which the used name or description applies to more than one individual. All such intentions are expressible by the use of descriptions, as the above shows. And since we are concerned here only with such intentions, we may talk about the speaker's intention description in every case in which the speaker succeeds in referring to an individual partly in virtue of his having a certain intention, even when the speaker would initially express that intention by the use of a name rather than by the use of a description.

The notion of an intention description can be used to state the necessary conditions of a speaker's making a statement which is about a particular individual, especially the second such condition put forth earlier. The speaker's intention is an intention to refer to *a certain individual* or *a particular individual* only if the complete expression of that intention states a relation between the speaker and that individual. But the expression of that intention will do this only if that individual is referred to in the expression of that intention. That is, the speaker must make reference to that individual in expressing his intention. However, in order for a complete expression of an intention to involve reference to a particular individual, that intention must be expressed by the use of a name or description which in fact applies to one and only one individual. This is not so when the speaker makes any other type of statement. With respect to any other type of statement, the speaker can use a name or a description which applies to more than one individual and still make a statement which is about a particular one of these individuals. For in all such cases the speaker's *intention* can be such as to render that statement a statement about a

---

[1] It is to be understood, of course, that names can occur in these descriptions, either by way of being used or by way of being mentioned.

particular one of those individuals. But this is not possible when the statement in question is *a statement which completely expresses the intention in question itself.* It is not possible for the speaker's intention to render that expression of the intention a statement which is about a particular individual if that expression does not already do so itself. There is nothing other than the intention itself that can perform this function. The expression of the intention itself must, so to speak, render itself an intention concerning that individual, since there is nothing beyond the intention which can do so. This is true not only for the intention itself but also for the statement which is a complete expression of that intention. There is nothing beyond this statement itself which can render this statement one which is about a particular individual. So this statement must, so to speak, render itself a statement which is about a particular individual. The only way in which the complete expression of the intention can do this is by involving a name or a description which applies to only one individual. Then the name or the description will *by itself* pick out that individual as the individual to whom the speaker has the relation stated in the expression of the intention (the relation of the speaker's trying to refer to that individual). The second necessary condition of the speaker's making a statement which is about a particular individual was stated at the end of Section 3 partly in terms of the speaker's intention being to refer to that individual. Now we can state this second necessary condition in the following way in terms of intention descriptions: in order for the speaker to make a statement which is about a particular individual, it is necessary that either the used (or uttered) name or description apply only to that individual or the speaker use that name or description with an intention whose complete expression involves an intention description which applies only to that individual.

Before moving to the next topic, we must note another important point. Complete expressions of intentions of the sort being discussed in this section can be about particular individuals even though they cannot themselves be rendered so by intentions in the way in which other statements can. This shows that there must be a way in which a statement can be about a particular individual independently of speaker's intentions. The only possible way in which this can occur is, as said above, by the used name or description itself being had by or satisfied by, and thus picking out, only one individual. This shows that the used name or description by itself renders a statement a statement which is about just one individual when the name or description applies to just one individual, at least in cases in which the speaker's intentions cannot do this. And this is at least part of what is claimed in the first part of the second necessary condition of a speaker's statement being about a particular individual.

5 *The relation between the uttered referring expression and the intention description*

The intention description must be individuating—that is, must be satisfied by one and only one individual—if the speaker is to succeed in referring in a case in which the uttered expression applies to more than one individual. Typically the uttered expression will itself be used or mentioned in the expression of the speaker's intention. Suppose, for example, that a speaker utters the name 'de Broglie' in an attempt to refer to an individual. His intention description may be 'the individual who originated wave mechanics and who is named "de Broglie" '. In fact, it may be the case that the intention description is individuating *only if* the uttered expression is used or mentioned in expressing the speaker's intention. In the above example, if there are two individuals who have the property of originating wave mechanics (independently of one another, perhaps), the above intention description may be satisfied by only one individual only if the intention description includes mention of the property of being named 'de Broglie'.

In general, what the speaker does when he uses a name or a description to refer to an individual is to utter some expression used in or mentioned in his intention description. He intends to refer to a certain individual. Which expression he utters in an attempt to refer to this individual will depend, for example, on what he believes about his hearers. In the above case, his intention description is 'the individual who originated wave mechanics and is named "de Broglie" '. If the speaker believes that his uttering the name 'de Broglie' will lead his hearers to identify the correct individual as the individual being referred to, then he may well utter that name in making his statement. But if, on the other hand, the speaker believes that his hearers do not know who bears the name 'de Broglie' but are familiar with the recent history of physics, he may instead utter the description 'the originator of wave mechanics' in making his statement. Again, the context may influence what expression he chooses to use in making his statement. For the use of a certain expression may, in that context, ensure that the hearers will identify the correct individual. But the context, in ensuring that the hearers will identify the correct individual, does not ensure that the speaker has succeeded in referring to that individual. It is the intention description which does that.

It is not always the case that the uttered expression is used or mentioned in the intention description. Let us suppose that the speaker wishes to refer to the individual who was the chairman of the Petrograd Soviet in 1917 and who created the Red Army. The speaker does not know what the name of this individual is but suspects (falsely, as it happens) that this individual's name is 'Zinoviev'. The speaker believes strongly that if 'Zinoviev' is the name of that individual, then the use of the name 'Zinoviev' in making his statement will ensure that the hearer identifies the correct individual as the individual being talked about, whereas the speaker believes that the use of the descriptions 'the Chairman of the Petrograd Soviet in 1917' and 'the creator of the Red Army', either alone or together, would not lead this hearer to identify the correct individual. For example, the speaker may believe that the hearer does not know that the individual in question was the Chairman of the Petrograd Soviet in 1917 and the creator of the Red Army. So the speaker uses 'Zinoviev' in making his statement. But it cannot be said that in this case the name 'Zinoviev' is mentioned in the speaker's intention description. The speaker does not intend to refer to the individual named 'Zinoviev'. The speaker suspects that 'Zinoviev' is a name of the individual to whom he is trying to refer and hopes that this is a name of that individual. At most what the speaker intends, with respect to the name 'Zinoviev', is to refer to the individual named 'Zinoviev' *if* that name is a name of the individual to whom he intends to refer. But then the individual to whom he intends to refer must be specified in the expression of his intention to refer to that individual in a way which does not involve the use or mention of the name 'Zinoviev'. He must be able to specify that individual without using or mentioning the name 'Zinoviev' in order to be able then to go on to say that he intends to refer to the individual named 'Zinoviev' if the individual to whom he intends to refer has that name. If he is asked who that individual to whom he intends to refer is, he cannot answer by saying 'Zinoviev', at least not finally; he must ultimately be able to answer this by using or mentioning some other expression—for instance, by saying "the individual who created the Red Army". So this is a case in which the used or uttered expression 'Zinoviev' is not used or mentioned in the speaker's intention description.

That the uttered name need not be used or mentioned in the speaker's intention description can also be shown in another way. Let us consider two cases. Case (1) is this. The speaker utters the name 'Pier Luigi Nervi'. When asked to whom he is thereby trying to refer, the speaker says "I intend thereby to refer to the individual named 'Pier Luigi Nervi' who was the engineer of the Madrid Hippodrome". Let us now suppose that there is one and only one individual named 'Pier Luigi Nervi' and that this individual was *not* the engineer of the Madrid Hippodrome. When the speaker is informed of this fact, he says "Then I do not know which individual—the individual named 'Pier Luigi Nervi' or the individual who was the engineer of the Madrid Hippodrome—I was trying to refer to". (He did refer to the individual named 'Pier Luigi Nervi' since he used that name and that name is the name of one and only one individual. But he did not succeed in referring to that individual because, as his reply shows, he was not trying to refer to that individual rather than the other.) Case (2) is this. The speaker utters the name 'Pier Luigi Nervi'. When asked to whom he is thereby trying to refer, the speaker says "I intend thereby to refer to the engineer of the Madrid Hippodrome". In fact the engineer of the Madrid Hippodrome does not have this name. When the speaker is informed of this fact, he says "I was trying to refer to the engineer of the Madrid Hippodrome, and I believed that 'Pier Luigi Nervi' was that individual's name". In case (2), unlike case (1), the inapplicability of the uttered name to a certain individual does not show that the speaker was not trying to refer to a particular individual. So to refer to an individual having that name cannot be what, or part of what, the speaker in case (2) intended in using that name.

The following objection might be made to this argument. It might be said that there is a type of case in which the speaker can intend to refer to an individual having a certain name and still be able to say truly that he was trying to refer to a particular individual even though that individual does not in fact have that name. This can be so if the speaker's intention description is of the type 'the individual who has a sufficient number of the following properties: $\emptyset$, $\mho$, . . . , and having the name "Harry S. Truman" '. An individual can have a sufficient number of these properties and thus be the individual to whom the speaker is trying to refer, without having the name 'Harry S. Truman'. Nevertheless, the name 'Harry S. Truman' is mentioned in the speaker's intention description. Therefore, that the speaker who uses the name 'Harry S. Truman' to refer to an individual can truly say that he was trying to refer to a certain particular individual even though that individual does not have the name 'Harry S. Truman' does not show that the name 'Harry S. Truman' is not mentioned in a complete expression of the speaker's intention in uttering that name.

It is true that the speaker's intention description can be of the form 'the individual who has a sufficient number of the following properties: $\emptyset$, $\mho$, Θ'. By holding that the speaker's intention description can and perhaps often does have this form, the Intention–Description Theory of Referring accounts for the apparent fact, mentioned by Searle and discussed in Chapter V, that a speaker can succeed in referring to an individual even if it turns out that that individual has only a sufficient number of the properties which the speaker believed that individual to have. The Abbreviation Theory of Referring accounts for this by saying that in such cases the abbreviated description has the form 'the individual who has a sufficient number of the properties $\emptyset$, $\mho$, Θ'. The Intention–Description Theory of Referring accounts for this by saying that in such cases the speaker's intention description has this form.

But there can still be cases which show that the uttered name is not necessarily mentioned in the speaker's intention description. Let us suppose that in case (2) the only way in which the speaker

THE INTENTION–DESCRIPTION THEORY OF REFERRING

is able to identify the individual to whom he is referring, other than by use of the name 'Pier Luigi Nervi', is by use of the description 'the engineer of the Madrid Hippodrome'. At most, his intention description is 'the individual who is the engineer of the Madrid Hippodrome and is named "Pier Luigi Nervi" '. Upon finding that no one individual has both properties, he further says "I was trying to refer to the individual who is the engineer of the Madrid Hippodrome". There are two individuals in this situation, one of whom bears the name 'Pier Luigi Nervi' and the other of whom is the engineer of the Madrid Hippodrome. If the speaker's intention description was of the suggested form 'the individual who has a sufficient number of the following properties: being named "Pier Luigi" and being the engineer of the Madrid Hippodrome', then in this case the speaker would still have to say that he did not know which of these individuals has a sufficient number of these properties, if any individual does, since each has exactly the same number of these properties as the other, namely one of these properties. But it is perfectly possible for a speaker to use the name 'Pier Luigi Nervi', be otherwise able to identify the individual to whom he is trying to refer only as the engineer of the Madrid Hippodrome, and still be able to say truly that he was trying to refer to the engineer upon finding that the engineer does not have the name 'Pier Luigi Nervi'. Since the speaker is still able to say truly that he was trying to refer to one of these individuals (the engineer) in this situation, his intention description in this case does not have the form 'the individual who has a sufficient number of the following properties: being named "Pier Luigi Nervi" and being the engineer of the Madrid Hippodrome'. Therefore, the name 'Pier Luigi Nervi' is not mentioned at all in the speaker's intention description. For, since the speaker's intention description does not have the form 'the individual who has a sufficient number of . . . ', it is only if that name is not mentioned at all in the speaker's intention description that the speaker can be trying to refer to an individual who does not in fact have that name. Thus, there can be cases in which the uttered expression is not used in or mentioned in the speaker's intention description.

It should be said at this point that when the speaker replies to the question "Whom do you mean?" or "Whom are you talking about?", his answer will usually not consist of a complete expression of his intention. In answering this question, the speaker is again trying to indicate to the questioner whom he is talking about, just as he was when he used a name or a description in making his statement. And now, as then, he may choose to employ for this purpose a part of the intention description which he believes will lead the hearer to identify the correct individual. Generally, he need not and does not use the entire intention description for this purpose. And it is possible that the expression which he does use for this purpose is not even part of his complete intention description, just as it is not necessary that the uttered expression be part of the intention description.[1]

A speaker can make a statement at time t_1 which is about a particular individual and, when asked at a later time t_2 whom he was referring to, the speaker can lie about this. That is, the speaker can say at t_2 that he was referring to a particular individual at t_1 while knowing at t_2 that he was not doing so at t_1. The Intention–Description Theory of Referring can account for the possibility of the speaker's lying about this by saying that the individual whom the speaker refers to at t_2 may not be identical with the individual who uniquely satisfied the speaker's intention description at t_1 and the speaker may know that this is the case. Of course an individual does not have to satisfy at t_2 the same intention description associated with the speaker's use of a name or description at t_1 in order to be at t_2 the individual whom the speaker was referring to at t_1. The individual only has to satisfy *that* intention description at t_1. Thus, the speaker may, at t_2, tell whom he was referring to at t_1 by using a name which that individual did not have at t_1 or a description which that individual did not satisfy at t_1.

If a speaker uses a referring expression in association with an intention description which does not uniquely apply to an individual, then the speaker may be said to be trying to refer to *an* individual but there is no individual to whom he is trying to refer. Hence, while the speaker is trying to refer to an individual, he is not trying to refer to a particular, specific individual.

[1] By saying that an expression is part of the intention description, I mean that the expression would be used or mentioned when the speaker expresses his complete intention.

6 The relation between the Intention–Description Theory of Referring and the Abbreviation Theory of Referring

The Abbreviation Theory of Referring says that when a speaker uses an expression to refer to a particular individual where that expression applies to more than one individual, the speaker succeeds in referring to that individual if and only if the uttered expression abbreviates a description which uniquely applies to that individual. For a name to abbreviate a description is for the token in question of that name to have the same meaning as that description. For a description to abbreviate a description is for the former to be part of the latter. The Intention–Description Theory of Referring says that in such cases the speaker succeeds in referring to that individual if and only if the intention description associated with the used or uttered expression is uniquely satisfied by that individual. So these two theories agree that in such cases the speaker succeeds in referring to an individual if and only if the used or uttered token stands in some relation to a description which is uniquely satisfied by a certain individual. They differ only over what that relation is. According to the Abbreviation Theory of Referring, that relation is one of synonymy (in the case of names) or a part–whole relation (in the case of descriptions). According to the Intention–Description Theory of Referring, that relation is as follows: *the token is used with a certain intention the complete expression of which requires the use of the description which is uniquely satisfied.* Let us call this relation—that is, the relation between the uttered expression and the description as that relation is specified by the Intention–Description Theory of Referring— "Relation R".

It was said in Section 1 of this chapter that the Intention–Description Theory of Referring can be construed in either of two ways: as part of the Abbreviation Theory of Referring; as independent of and an alternative to the Abbreviation Theory of Referring. Now I want to explain more fully how it can be construed in each of these ways.

In the chapters on the Abbreviation Theory of Referring, it was said that this theory holds that tokens of names are used to stand for descriptions. But of course each uttered token could stand for any one of a number of descriptions. And it must be explained

(i) why the token stands for one description rather than another, and (ii) what it is for the token to stand for one description rather than another. The Intention–Description Theory of Referring can be regarded as being an answer to each of these questions: (i) the token stands for this description rather than that because it is this description rather than that which stands in Relation R to this token; (ii) what it is for this token to stand for one description rather than another is for this description rather than another to be the one (or a one) which stands in Relation R to that token. An analogous problem arises, on the Abbreviation Theory of Referring, for uttered *descriptions* in those cases in which the uttered descriptions do not each apply to just one individual; (iii) why does the uttered description abbreviate this particular description of which it is a part rather than some other description of which it is a part; (iv) what is it for one description to abbreviate another? The Intention–Description Theory of Referring can be regarded as being an answer to each of these questions also: (iii) the uttered description abbreviates whatever description it stands in Relation R to; (iv) for an uttered description to abbreviate another description is for the first to stand in Relation R to the second.[1]

Thus, the Intention–Description Theory of Referring can be regarded in the way just described as an essential and very large part of the complete Abbreviation Theory of Referring. But it can also instead be regarded as independent of and an alternative to the Abbreviation Theory of Referring. It provides a solution to the problem set forth in Chapter I without necessarily claiming that names and descriptions are abbreviations. It claims that the speaker succeeds in referring in cases of ambiguous reference if and only if the uttered expression (which in these cases applies to more than one individual) stands in Relation R to a description which is uniquely satisfied. Then the speaker succeeds in referring to the individual who satisfies the uttered expression and uniquely

[1] But it should be noted that in view of what was said in the previous section (Section 5) about the possibility of the uttered expression's being neither used in nor mentioned in the speaker's intention description, if we do regard the Intention—Description Theory of Referring as a part of the Abbreviation Theory of Referring, then it is possible for a name to abbreviate a description in which the name is not mentioned and it is possible for a description to abbreviate a description of which the first description is not a part, that is, in the expression of which the first is not used.

satisfies (that is, is the only individual who satisfies) the description to which the uttered expression stands in Relation R. Nothing is said here about what the meaning of the uttered expression is, nor is it even claimed that the uttered expression must have a meaning. Nothing is said here about names and descriptions being abbreviations of descriptions, being synonymous with descriptions, or being parts of descriptions. The Abbreviation Theory of Referring talks of names and descriptions as being abbreviations and as being synonymous with or part of the abbreviated descriptions.[1] Since the Intention–Description Theory of Referring can provide a solution to the problem of ambiguous reference described in Chapter I without claiming that names and descriptions are abbreviations and synonymous with or part of descriptions, the Intention–Description Theory of Referring can be regarded as independent of and an alternative to the Abbreviation Theory of Referring.

One difficulty with regarding the two theories as independent of one another and as alternatives is this. It may in fact be true that when a name is used in such a way as to stand in Relation R to a description, that name is synonymous with that description. This may be true in virtue of what it is for a word to have a meaning. Consider the case of ambiguous terms which are not names. It is clear that a speaker can use an ambiguous term in just one of its meanings. The same is true for an ambiguous sentence: the speaker can be making one of the statements that can be made by uttering this sentence rather than another when he utters that sentence in a given case. And it seems that what makes this a case of the speaker's making this statement rather than that statement, where each can be made by uttering this sentence, is the speaker's intending to make that statement rather than the other statement. Of course, the speaker must be able to express the intention in question by the use of a sentence which is not itself ambiguous. Otherwise, the same problem would arise with respect to the sentence which the speaker used to express his intention; and it would not be clear from that sentence which statement the speaker

---

[1] It might be claimed that the Abbreviation Theory can be formulated in such a way as to avoid holding that names have meanings and are synonymous with descriptions. But such a formulation would, I think, be substantially the same as the Intention–Description Theory of Referring.

intended to make. If an ambiguous word or an ambiguous sentence is used *in* a particular one of its meanings, the token of that word or sentence which the speaker uses may be said to *have* that meaning. When a speaker means this or that in using an ambiguous word or sentence, the used token of the ambiguous word or sentence *has* that meaning. If this is so, then if, as just suggested, a token of the ambiguous word has a certain meaning in virtue of being used with a certain intention, and if it is said by the Intention–Description Theory of Referring that a certain token of a name stands in Relation R to a certain description, it follows from this that that name-token *has* the same meaning as that description if that name is an ambiguous word, that is, if that name has meanings to begin with. And this would follow even if the Intention–Description Theory of Referring does not use the words 'abbreviation', 'synonymy', and so on, to describe the relation between the name-token and the description.

It might be said that at least some names are ambiguous and that the sentences in which they occur are ambiguous sentences on the following grounds. What it is for a sentence to be ambiguous is just this: the sentence can be used to make more than one statement. But sentences containing names which are names of more than one individual can, merely in virtue of containing those names, be used to make more than one statement in our sense of the term 'statement'. For a given one of these sentences can be used to say something about at least several different individuals—those individuals who bear the name contained by that sentence—and thus can be used to make at least several different statements. So on this view of what an ambiguous word is—namely, a word which is such that its being contained by a sentence allows the sentence to be used to make more than one statement—names which are had by more than one individual are ambiguous words. And if such names are ambiguous words, than it seems that if a token of such a name is used in such a way as to stand in Relation R to a description, then that token *has* the same meaning as that description, on the theory suggested above of what it is for a token of an ambiguous word to have a certain meaning. And this is so regardless of whether the Intention–Description Theory of Referring claims that this is so or uses the terms 'meaning', 'synonymy', and so on. This follows merely from the nature of ambiguous words and the nature of Relation R. Thus, it might be said, what the Intention–Description Theory of Referring shows is that name-tokens in many cases do have the same meanings as descriptions. Hence this theory is part of or is largely identical with the Abbreviation Theory of Referring, even if this theory does not use the same terms—such as 'abbreviation', 'synonymy', and so on—to describe the relation between such name-tokens and descriptions. For the holding of Relation R between such a name-token and a description results in that name-token's having the same meaning as that description. Relation R is precisely the type of relation which gives a token of an ambiguous word a meaning.

It might be objected to this that an uttered token of a *description* which is satisfied by more than one individual—for example, a token of the description 'the Senator'—can stand in Relation R to another description—for example, to the description 'the senior Senator from New York'—and yet that token does not thereby have the same meaning as the description to which the token stands in Relation R. This token of 'the Senator' does not *mean* what the expression 'the senior Senator from New York' means. Instead, this token means exactly what every other token of 'the Senator' means, regardless of what descriptions these tokens stand in Relation R to. Hence, a token's standing in Relation R to a description does not thereby come to have the same meaning as that description. Hence, a name-token standing in Relation R to a description does not necessarily thereby come to have the same meaning as that description. It will perhaps then be replied that this objection is not sound because a name-token and a descrip-tion-token are not similar in a crucial respect, even if both the name and the description (of which these are tokens) apply to more than one individual. The respect in which they are dissimilar is this: the name is an ambiguous word while the description is not ambiguous. For example, the description of 'the Senator' does not have more than one meaning even if more than one individual is a senator. It is only when the expression of which the token in question is a token is an ambiguous word or phrase that the tokens of this expression come to have certain meanings by stand-ing in Relation R to certain descriptions. Thus, since names which are had by more than one individual are ambiguous words, their tokens come to have meanings through standing in Relation R to descriptions. But since descriptions which are satisfied by more than one individual are not ambiguous phrases, their tokens cannot come to have meanings in virtue of standing in Relation R to descriptions; these tokens do not satisfy a necessary condition of coming thereby to have meanings, namely being tokens of ambiguous words or phrases. So tokens of such names can still come to have meanings in this way even if tokens of descriptions do not do so. And it must be pointed out that the Abbreviation Theory of Referring does not claim that tokens of such descriptions do come to have meanings in this way. This theory claims only that tokens of such names come to have meanings in this way.

But this is not correct. It is true that the case of descriptions cannot be used to show that in the case of names which are ambiguous words, tokens of such names cannot come to have meaning in this way. For it is true that descriptions do not satisfy the supposed necessary condition described above, namely being ambiguous words or phrases, this being allegedly a necessary condition of a token of the expression in question coming to have meaning in this way. But nevertheless, the case of descriptions which apply to more than one individual can be used to show that names which are had by more than one individual are not therefore ambiguous words. It was said that an ambiguous word or phrase was one whose presence in a sentence allows that sentence to be used to make more than one statement. And it was said that a name which is had by more than one individual is ambiguous because its presence in a sentence allows that sentence to be used to make more than one statement—in our sense of 'statement'—namely a different statement about each individual who has that name. But it is also true that a description which is satisfied by more than one individual is such that its presence in a sentence allows that sentence to be used to make a statement about each individual who satisfies that description. For example, the sentence 'The United States Senator is in Washington today' can be used to make statements about quite a number of different individuals. So if the presence of a word or phrase in a sentence allowing that sentence to be used to make more than one statement (in our sense of 'statement') makes that word or phrase ambiguous, then the description 'the United States Senator' would be ambiguous. But this description is not ambiguous; this description does not have more than one meaning. And even if it does have more than one meaning—for example, it might be said to mean "the Senator who is a member of the Federal Government" and "the Senator who resides in the United States" (which is true of state senators too)—this description certainly does not have as many meanings as there are individuals about whom this description can be used to make statements, as would be the case for names if the Abbreviation Theory of Referring is true. So the number of statements that can be made by using a certain referring expression is not a criterion of how many meanings that referring expression has. Consequently, it is not true that the fact that the presence of a word or a phrase in a sentence allows that sentence to be used to make more than one statement shows that that word or phrase is ambiguous. Consequently, the argument given previously does not show that names which are had by more than one individual are ambiguous words. Hence this argument does not show that such names fulfil the alleged necessary condition of their tokens coming to have meaning through standing in Relation R to descriptions.

For this reason, it is preferable to regard the Intention–Description Theory of Referring as independent of and an alternative to the Abbreviation Theory of Referring. For there is no reason to say that names have *descriptive* meanings and, in particular, that they are synonymous with certain descriptions. Moreover, we can still give a "descriptivist" solution to the problem of ambiguous reference set forth in Chapter I and can describe the relation between names and descriptions on the one hand and other descriptions on the other without claiming that names have meanings. If it is true that names do have meaning and descriptions do abbreviate other descriptions, however, the Intention–Description of Referring would claim that it gives the correct account of what it is for a name-token to be used in a certain meaning, why the name-token has that meaning rather than some other, what it is for a description which is part of many descriptions to abbreviate only one of the latter, and why the uttered description abbreviates this description rather than that description. Thus I am claiming that the Intention–Description Theory of Referring is true, that there is no reason to believe that names have *descriptive* meanings, and hence that there is no reason to believe that the Abbreviation

Theory of Referring is true. But I also claim that if the Abbreviation Theory of Referring were true, it would have to include the Intention–Description Theory of Referring as an essential and very large part.

7 *The use of* 'The'

I have said that the descriptive referring phrase 'the Senator' can be used to refer successfully to more than one individual, that is, that statements about different individuals can be made by using this phrase. It seems to have been believed by some people, notably Russell (in his Theory of Descriptions), that whenever the term 'the' is used in a referring phrase such as 'the Senator', it means "the one and only". If this were so, then it would not be possible for two speakers to use 'the Senator' at the same time to make statements about different individuals. For if there are two individuals who are senators, neither is the one and only senator. Since 'the Senator' can be used to refer successfully to just one of these individuals, 'the' does not mean "the one and only" in descriptive referring phrases. Moreover, it is clear that 'the' does not signify that the speaker is referring to just one individual, since the description 'the Senators' can be used to refer to several individuals.

What the term 'the' indicates in most cases in which it occurs in a descriptive referring phrase is that the speaker is referring to a particular individual or to particular individuals, that is, that the speaker is making a statement which is about such an individual or individuals. The speaker is indicating that his statement is true only if certain particular individuals have certain properties, not if just any individual satisfying the descriptive referring phrase has certain properties. This use of 'the' is to be contrasted with the use of 'a'. When the speaker says "A Senator is in Washington today", his statement is true if and only if any senator is in Washington today. But if the speaker says "The Senator is in Washington today", he indicates that what he says is true if and only if a certain particular Senator is in Washington today. This can be put by saying that the statement "The Senator is in Washington today" is about a particular individual.

There is at least one exception to this thesis about the use of 'the' in phrases of the form 'the ——'. A speaker may say, for example, "The Roman Senator was expected to contribute to various charitable causes" and is not thereby talking about any particular Roman Senator. Instead, the speaker is talking about the class of Roman Senators or about each member of that class. So here 'the' does not indicate that the speaker is talking about a certain particular individual.

8 *Mentioning the properties associated with the uttered expression*

We have seen that the uttered expression need not be one which is used or mentioned in the speaker's intention description (see Section 5 of this chapter). For example, a speaker can use the name 'Gauss' without it being the case that he intends to refer to an individual named 'Gauss', that is, without it being in this way part of his intention that the individual be named 'Gauss'. For the speaker may only suspect that the individual to whom he is trying to refer is named 'Gauss' and may claim that it does not follow from an individual's not being named 'Gauss' that that individual is not the one to whom he is trying to refer.

Let us use the phrase 'the properties associated with the uttered expression' in the following way: if the name 'Gauss' is uttered, then the property associated with this uttered expression is the property of being named 'Gauss'; if the description 'the individual who is Ø' is the uttered expression, then the property associated with this expression is the property Ø. What was said in the preceding paragraph can now be put in the following way: the properties associated with the uttered expression need not be mentioned in the complete expression of the speaker's intention in uttering that expression.

But it is also true that the properties associated with the uttered expression must be had by an individual if that individual is to be successfully referred to by the speaker. This was shown in Section 2 of this chapter. This has the following consequence. Let us suppose that the speaker utters the name 'Gauss' and that his intention description has the form 'the individual who has a sufficient number of the following properties: Ø, Θ, and having the name "Gauss" '. In this situation, the property "having the name

'Gauss' " is in a different position from that of the properties Ø and Θ. For the speaker could successfully refer to an individual in this situation by using the name 'Gauss' even if that individual did not have the property Θ. The individual could have Ø and the property of being named 'Gauss', and it might be sufficient for the individual to have only these two properties without having Θ as well. But it is not possible for the speaker to refer successfully in this situation to an individual who does not have the name 'Gauss'. Consequently, the property of having the name 'Gauss' is not like the properties Ø and Θ. The individual successfully referred to must have the name 'Gauss' but need not have Ø or Θ (although perhaps he must have either Ø or Θ). Thus, even if the speaker's intention description is of the form 'the individual who has a sufficient number of . . . ', not all of the properties mentioned in this intention description are necessarily in the same position as one another. *It is still possible, even with an intention description of this form, that there are certain properties which an individual must have in order to be the individual to whom the speaker has successfully referred.*

9 *Types of theories of referring*

The Intention–Description Theory of Referring is a descriptivist theory of referring because it holds that every case of successful referring essentially involves a certain relation between the used expression and a description. But it holds that referring expressions, especially names, need not be regarded as having descriptive meaning. The successful referring use of a name is on this theory not a purely denotative matter. But it does not follow from this that the successful referring use of a name is partly a connotative matter. There is a third possibility—that represented by the Intention–Description Theory of Referring. According to this theory, the successful referring use of a name does not involve or depend on any connotation which the name itself has but does essentially involve the presence of something—the intention description—which does have connotative meaning.

10 *Two senses of 'refer' and of 'talking about someone'*

The term 'refer' seems to be used in two different ways in ordinary discourse. The question "To whom is the speaker referring?" can, and perhaps in the majority of cases is, taken to be the question "Whom is his statement about?" In this first sense of 'refer', a speaker has referred to an individual if he has made a statement which *is* in fact about that individual.

Let us now suppose that the speaker says "Truman is the former Senate majority leader". A hearer, knowing that Harry S. Truman was never the Senate majority leader and wondering whom the speaker was trying to make a statement about, might ask "To whom is he referring?" and be told "to the current President". This reply in this type of situation tells the hearer that the speaker is trying to make a statement about the current President. In this second sense of 'refer', the speaker refers to whichever individual he is *trying* to make a statement about. Thus, in this second sense of 'refer', the speaker is referring to whichever individual he is trying to refer to in the first sense of 'refer'.

Another expression which has two senses of just these types is the expression 'talking about someone'. The question "Whom is he talking about?" can be properly answered by telling whom it is that the speaker's statement is in fact about, whether or not the speaker knows that the statement is about that individual (rather than the one whom he believes it to be about), or by telling whom it is that the speaker is trying to make a statement about, whether or not he succeeds in doing so. Thus, the speaker who says "Truman is a former Senate majority leader" with the intention of making a statement about the current President may be said to be talking about the current President. In this kind of case, the *speaker* is *talking about* the current President, but his *statement* is not *about* the current President.[1] That there are two senses of 'talking about someone' is also shown by the fact that both in a case in which the speaker can truly say only "That's what I meant" and in a case in which he can also truly say "That's what I said", the speaker can truly say "That's whom I was talking about".

The Intention–Description Theory of Referring accounts for the existence of these two senses of these two expressions in the following way: when the speaker makes a statement by using a token of a name or a description which applies to only one individual or which applies to more than one individual one of whom uniquely satisfies the speaker's intention description, then the

[1] It is assumed here that the correct President is not named 'Truman'.

speaker has referred to that individual and has talked about that individual in the first senses of these expressions. If the speaker's intention description is uniquely satisfied by an individual different from any individual to whom the used expression applies, then the speaker may have referred to that individual and has talked about that individual in the second sense of each of these expressions. Thus, a speaker can refer to or talk about an individual in one of these senses without referring to or talking about that individual in the other of these senses.

Even though the expressions of 'referring' and 'talking about someone' each have two senses which are similar in these ways, these expressions do not seem to be synonymous with one another. For there seems to be at least one sort of case in which a speaker can be truly described as talking about a certain individual without being truly describable as referring to that individual. The case is this: the speaker wishes to convey information about a certain individual to the hearer; the speaker correctly believes that the hearer believes that this individual has the name 'Smith'; the speaker further correctly believes that this individual does not in fact have the name 'Smith'; and the speaker also believes that if he uses the name 'Smith' in making a statement, the hearer will believe that the statement is about the individual about whom the speaker wishes to convey information; so the speaker utters the words 'Smith was born in Denmark' in order to convey to the hearer that the individual in question was born in Denmark. There is an intention description in this situation because the speaker is using the term 'Smith' with a certain intention which concerns a particular individual, namely the intention of leading the hearer to identify that individual as the individual whom the speaker's statement is about. And it seems that the speaker can be truly described as talking about the individual who uniquely satisfies the intention description. Let us now suppose that a third hearer and a fourth hearer both know that the name 'Smith' is not the name of anyone and that they know that the speaker also knows that the name 'Smith' is not the name of anyone. The third hearer could correctly use the expression 'talking about someone' here; he could appropriately ask the fourth hearer "Whom is he talking about?" to find out what the speaker's intention description is or at least which individual satisfies that intention description. And the fourth hearer could correctly reply "He is talking about Argentina's most prominent lawyer". Since this is so, the speaker is talking about the individual in question. But it would not be correct for the third hearer to express this question by saying "Whom is he referring to?" The speaker is not referring to anyone, nor is he even trying to refer to someone. He is doing something quite different—something which will be discussed in the next section (Section 11). Since the speaker is, in this case, talking about that individual but not referring, in any sense of 'referring', to that individual, the expressions 'referring to someone' and 'talking about someone' are not synonymous.

In the above case, the speaker used a name 'Smith' which cannot be used in making a statement about the individual in question. For the name 'Smith' is not that individual's name. It seems that a speaker can be referring to an individual, in the ordinary use of the term 'refer', only if the speaker is making a statement which is about an individual, asking a question which is about an individual (at least in part), giving an order which is about an individual, expressing a wish or a hope which concerns an individual, or is trying to do one of these things. In the above case, what the speaker does is very similar to making a statement about an individual, but it is not in fact the making of a statement about an individual nor is the speaker trying to do this. For this reason the speaker does not refer to this individual in the above case.[1]

11 Referring to an individual and referring a hearer to an individual

In the previous section a case was described in which the speaker used a name which he knew was not a name of the individual in

[1] There are other sorts of linguistic actions which can involve the use of names or descriptions—for example, addressing a question, a request, or a command to an individual, calling to an individual, calling an individual over to one, and so on. Each action of these sorts can also involve intention descriptions, just as using a name or a description to make a statement can. But these actions do not seem to involve referring in the ordinary use of 'refer'. If the speaker calls to an individual, the individual might say "Are you calling me?" but not "Are you referring to me?" It seems that referring occurs only in connection with linguistic actions on the level of making statements, asking questions, giving commands, and so on, in the way indicated above, rather than such actions as addressing a question or a command which are preparatory to the performance of actions which are on the level on which referring to an individual takes place.

question in order to convey information about that individual to a hearer. The speaker used the name 'Smith', even though he knew that this individual's name is not 'Smith'. The speaker believed that the use of the name 'Smith' would lead the hearer to identify the correct individual as the one about whom the speaker was trying to convey information. And it was said that in such a case the speaker is not referring, or even trying to refer, to that individual. But then what is the speaker trying to do, other than trying to convey information about that individual to the hearer? What the speaker is trying to do is to lead the hearer to identify a certain individual as the one about whom the information is being conveyed—or, as we may put it, he is trying to refer the hearer to the individual. Referring the hearer to the individual is part of conveying information to the hearer about that individual.

Referring the hearer to an individual can occur at the same time as, and by use of the same means as, the speaker's referring to that individual. In a typical case, there are many expressions which a speaker can use in referring to a given individual. And very often the speaker chooses to use the one which he believes has the best chance of referring the hearer to the individual to whom the speaker is referring. But if both of these activities—referring to an individual and referring a hearer to an individual—can occur at the same time and through the use of the same expressions, what reason is there to say that these are two different activities? After all, it might be said that a speaker refers to an individual if and only if he refers the hearer to that individual and that the two activities—referring to an individual and referring a hearer to an individual—are in fact identical with one another.

However, these are two distinct activities. That they are distinct can be shown in the following ways. First, it is possible for the activity of referring to an individual to take place without the activity of referring a hearer to an individual to take place. A speaker refers to an individual if he makes a statement which is about that individual. (a) But a speaker can make a statement which is about an individual without any hearer's identifying that individual as the one whom the statement is about. For example, the speaker may mistakenly believe that the hearer is still in the room and so utters the words 'William Steinberg will make appearances in Europe next month' where the associated intention description is 'the current conductor of the Boston Symphony Orchestra'. The speaker thereby makes a statement which is about William Steinberg. But since no hearer is present on this occasion, no hearer identifies William Steinberg or anyone else as the individual whom the statement is about. Since the statement is nevertheless about William Steinberg, the speaker has referred to William Steinberg. Thus, the speaker can succeed in referring to an individual without succeeding in referring a hearer to an individual. Hence, referring to an individual is different from referring a hearer to an individual. (b) Conversely, it is possible to refer a hearer to an individual without referring to that individual. Let us now suppose that there are several hearers and that the speaker utters the same sentence as in (a) in association with the same intention description. One hearer identifies the current conductor of the Boston Symphony as the individual whom the speaker is talking about, while the other incorrectly identifies some other man as the individual whom the speaker is talking about. The speaker has referred to only one individual. Consequently, since each hearer has been referred to a different individual, it is possible for a speaker to refer a hearer to an individual to whom the speaker is not referring (in which case the speaker unintentionally refers that hearer to that individual). Since referring a hearer to an individual can take place without the speaker's referring to that individual, referring to an individual and referring a hearer to an individual are two different activities.

The case described in the previous section and at the beginning of this section also can be used to show this. A necessary condition of making a statement which is about an individual is that the speaker use a name or description which applies to that individual. Therefore, when the speaker uses the name 'Smith' in this case, he does not succeed in referring to that individual. But he does succeed in referring the hearer to that individual. Consequently, referring to an individual and referring a hearer to an individual are two different activities.

One of the main differences between these two different activities is this. A speaker cannot succeed in referring a hearer to an individual unless a hearer does in fact come to believe that a certain individual is the one about whom the speaker has made a statement or is trying to make a statement. For referring a hearer to an individual to take place, a hearer must do something. This can be put by saying that referring a hearer to an individual is a "hearer–dependent activity". But referring to an individual is a "hearer–independent activity". Nothing need be done by any hearer in order for a speaker to succeed in referring to an individual. *That is, a statement's being about a particular individual rather than any other individual is independent of anything any hearer does or does not do.* There is a similarity here between the pair of activities "referring to an individual and referring a hearer to an individual" on the one hand and the pair of activities "asserting that *p* and giving the hearer to understand that *p*" on the other hand. There is also a similarity to "explaining something" and "explaining something to somebody". The first member of each pair is hearer–independent, while the second member of each pair is hearer–dependent.

Another difference between referring to an individual and referring a hearer to an individual, and one which is closely related to the first difference, is this. Whether or not a speaker succeeds in referring a hearer to an individual depends in part on the hearer's beliefs. For example, if the speaker uses the name 'Smith' in an attempt to refer a hearer to an individual, then if this attempt is to be successful, the hearer must believe either that 'Smith' is one of the names of that individual or that the speaker is trying to refer, or to refer him, to that individual, or both of these. But whether or not the speaker succeeds in referring to an individual depends not at all on any hearer's beliefs but instead on the relation between the used expression and, in many cases, the intention description on the one hand and the state of the world on the other. It depends, that is, on whether there is one and only one individual to whom either the used expression alone or the used expression and the intention description together apply.

However, referring to an individual and referring a hearer to an individual are similar with respect to part of the role of the speaker's intention description. For the speaker to *succeed* in either referring to an individual or referring a hearer to an individual or both, the speaker must be *trying* to do this. And in order to be trying to do this, the speaker must have a certain sort of intention in uttering the used expression. His intention must be an intention whose expression contains what I have been calling an "intention description". For his intention must be an intention to do something with respect to the individual. So his intention must pick out that individual in virtue of its complete expression containing an intention description which is uniquely satisfied by that individual. Thus, in order to succeed in either referring to an individual or referring a hearer to an individual or both, a speaker must use an expression in association with an intention description which is uniquely satisfied by that individual. But there is still an important difference between these two activities with respect to the role of the intention description. It was said in Section 3 that in the circumstances that the used expression applies to more than one individual, then a sufficient condition of the speaker's succeeding in referring to one of those individuals is that the intention description apply to one and only one of those individuals. But the analogue to this is not true for referring a hearer to an individual. Given that the used expression applies to several individuals, it is not a sufficient condition of the speaker's succeeding in referring a hearer to one of these individuals that the associated intention description be uniquely satisfied by one of these individuals. For it is also necessary that the hearer come to identify that individual as the one being talked about.

We have already seen in Section 2 that a necessary condition of a speaker's succeeding in referring to an individual is that the used or uttered expression apply to that individual. This gives rise to another difference between referring to an individual and referring a hearer to an individual. For it is not a necessary condition of a speaker's succeeding in referring a hearer to an individual that the speaker use an expression which applies to that individual. As we saw above, a speaker can, for example, refer a hearer to an individual by using a name which is not a name of that individual.

12 *Referring a hearer to an individual and conveying information about that individual*

Since a speaker can refer a hearer to an individual and thereby convey information to that hearer about that individual by using an expression which does not apply to that individual, the speaker can do this by using any referring expression whatever. This is so if the hearer has the proper beliefs such that these beliefs and the used expression lead the hearer to identify that individual as the individual being talked about. Therefore the speaker can use for this purpose an expression which applies to one and only one individual and furthermore not to the individual to whom the speaker is trying to refer the hearer. Let us suppose that the name 'Abel' is a name of one and only one individual and that the speaker utters the name 'Abel' for the purpose of referring the hearer to an individual whose only name is 'Galois'. Let us further suppose that the sentence which the speaker utters is 'Abel developed the theory of groups'. What the speaker is trying to do here is to convey to the hearer the information that Galois developed the theory of groups, since he believes that his use of 'Abel' will lead the hearer to identify Galois as the individual being talked about. Now suppose that the hearer does identify Galois as the individual being talked about, that Galois did develop the theory of groups, and that Abel did not develop the theory of groups. In this situation the speaker has conveyed to the hearer the information that Galois developed the theory of groups. But the speaker has done this not only by making a statement which is not about Galois (since Galois does not bear the name 'Abel') but also by making a statement which is false. That is, the speaker conveys something true to the hearer by making a statement which is false.

There are two different kinds of cases in which a speaker can succeed in conveying information about an individual to a hearer without referring to that individual. The first kind of case is that already discussed, namely that in which the speaker refers the hearer to the individual without trying to refer to the individual. For example, the speaker uses an expression which he believes not to apply to the individual in question but which he believes will lead the hearer to identify the individual in question as the one being talked about. The second kind of case is that in which the speaker attempts to refer to that individual but does not succeed in doing so. Yet the hearer knows on other grounds which individual it is to whom the speaker is trying to refer. Thus the hearer is referred to that individual without the speaker having succeeded in referring to that individual.

13 *Cases in which the used expression constitutes the intention description*

It has already been said that in a case in which just one individual has the used name or satisfies the used description, the speaker's statement is about that individual. If the intention description associated with this used expression also is uniquely satisfied by this individual, then the speaker has succeeded in referring to that individual. If this intention description is not uniquely satisfied by that individual, then the speaker has inadvertently or unintentionally referred to that individual.

There are cases in which it is not only sufficient that only one individual have the used name or satisfy the used description in order for the speaker to have referred to an individual but also necessary that only one individual do so in order for the speaker to have succeeded in referring to a particular individual. One type of case is this: the intention description is such that it can be satisfied by only one individual at a time. For example, the intention description might be 'the only individual to have flown across the Atlantic prior to 1925'. But there is another type of case of this general kind in which it is necessary that there be only one individual to whom the used expression applies, not because of the nature of the intention description, but because of the relation between the used expression and the intention description. These are cases which I shall call "cases in which the used expression constitutes the intention description".

14 *Selective referring and non-selective referring*

Cases in which the used expression constitutes the intention description are those in which (i) if the used expression is a name, then the only property mentioned by the intention description is the property of having that name, and (ii) if the used expression is a description, then the only properties mentioned by the intention description are the properties mentioned by the used description. In such cases, the speaker will not have succeeded in referring to anyone if there is more than one individual who has the used name or to whom the used description applies. For in such cases the speaker intends to make a statement about the one and only one individual who has the used name or satisfies the used description. In such cases, the speaker intends to refer to *whoever it is* that is the only individual to have the used name or satisfy the used description. These cases are such that the intention description does not play any role in determining *whom it is* the speaker has made a statement about, although it plays a role in determining whether or not the speaker has succeeded in referring to a particular individual. We have seen that in cases in which the used expression applies to more than one individual, the intention description can determine which of these individuals the statement is about. Let us call these cases—that is, cases in which, if the used expression applies to more than one individual, the intention description can *select* one of those individuals as the one whom the statement is about—"cases of selective referring". Cases of selective referring are those in which the intention description goes beyond the used expression, even if the intention description does not select an individual because in fact the used expression does apply to only one individual. But in other cases, the intention description does not go beyond the used expression itself—does not mention properties beyond those already mentioned by using or (in the case of names) involved in the use of the uttered expression—and hence cannot assist in selecting the individual whom the speaker's statement is about. Let us call such cases "cases of non-selective referring". In cases of selective referring, the speaker's intention description selects which individual the speaker's statement is about from the group consisting of the individuals to whom the used expression applies. The intention description does this by mentioning *further* properties—in addition to those indicated by the used expression—which the individual must also have in order to be the individual whom the statement is about. But since in cases of non-selective referring, the intention description does not mention such further properties, the intention description cannot select an individual from this group. Hence the speaker succeeds in referring to an individual in one of these cases only if this group has only one member—that is, only if the used expression applies to only one individual.

In all cases in which the used expression applies to only one individual, the speaker's statement is about that one individual, regardless of what the intention description is or to whom the intention description applies. There are three sorts of cases here. (1) The intention description does apply to the one individual to whom the used expression applies and only to that individual. There are two sub-classes in this group: (1*a*) cases in which the used expression constitutes the intention description; (1*b*) cases in which the used expression does not constitute the intention description. (2) The intention description does not apply to the one individual to whom the used expression applies or else does apply to that individual but not only to that individual. In all cases of type (1), the speaker intended to refer to the individual to whom the used expression applies, and, of course, succeeds in doing so, while in cases of type (2) the speaker refers inadvertently or unintentionally to that individual. In cases of type (1*a*) and in cases of type (2) the intention description does not play any role in determining whom the speaker's statement is about. But there is a very great difference between these two types of cases. For in cases of type (1*a*) the speaker *intended* to make a statement about the individual whom his statement is in fact about, while in cases of type (2) this is not so.

One major difference between cases of selective referring and cases of non-selective referring is this. In a case of non-selective referring, the speaker is attempting to refer to the individual to whom the *used expression* uniquely applies, *whoever that individual is, that is, whatever other properties that individual has* (besides those involved in the used expression). But in a case of selective referring, the speaker is not trying to refer to *whomever it is* that satisfies the used expression. The speaker is trying to refer to an individual who has certain other properties as well.

However, cases of selective referring do have a property which is analogous to the property of cases of non-selective referring just described. In a case of selective referring, the speaker is trying to refer to the individual to whom the *intention description* uniquely applies, *whoever that individual is, that is, whatever other properties that individual has, or, to put this in another way, whoever else that individual turns out to be.* Since cases of non-selective referring are, by the meaning of the phrase 'cases of non-selective referring', cases in which the used expression constitutes the intention description, both cases of selective referring and cases of non-selective referring can be described in this way: *the speaker is attempting to refer to the individual to whom the intention description uniquely applies, whoever that individual is or whoever else that individual is.* In each type of case, if an individual has certain properties, there are no grounds on which the speaker can justifiably deny that this is the individual whom his statement is about, whatever other properties that individual may turn out to have.

In a case of non-selective referring, the used expression constitutes the intention description, so that if an individual satisfies one of these, that same individual will satisfy the other too. In a case of selective referring, an individual can satisfy the used expression without satisfying the intention description. Of course, it is possible in both types of cases that more than one individual satisfies both the used expression and the intention description, in which case the speaker has not succeeded in referring to anyone. It is also possible in a case of selective referring for the class of individuals who satisfy the used expression to be non-overlapping with the class of individuals who satisfy the intention description, particularly in a case in which the property mentioned by the used expression is not mentioned in the intention description or in a case in which the intention description has the form 'the individual who has a sufficient number of . . . '.

Someone may doubt that there ever are any cases of non-selective referring even though such cases are possible in principle. So here are two examples of such cases. (1) Suppose that the speaker remembers that someone whom he justifiably believed to have spoken the truth told him that John Smith was the first man to have flown across the Atlantic. But the speaker does not remember who told him this. And the speaker does not remember anything else about the individual who was the first man to have flown across the Atlantic, except that his name was 'John Smith'. If the speaker then says to someone else "John Smith was the first man to fly across the Atlantic", this is a case of non-selective referring. For if the hearer says "Which John Smith are you referring to?", there is no way in which the speaker can select one of the several John Smiths who do or did exist as the one about whom he was talking. (2) Suppose that the speaker makes a statement by using a descriptive referring phrase which mentions every property that the speaker believes to belong to the individual about whom he is talking. For example, the speaker might say "The French emperor who was born in Corsica and invaded Russia in 1812 had several brothers and sisters". If all that the speaker knows or believes about the individual about whom he is talking is that this individual was a French emperor who was born in Corsica and invaded Russia in 1812, then if there are two individuals having these properties (perhaps co-emperors), there is no property on which the speaker can base a claim to have made a statement about one of these individuals rather than the other. Hence this is a case of non-selective referring.

The following objection might be made to the second of these cases.[1] It might be said that even if there were two individuals who were French emperors born in Corsica and who invaded Russia in 1812, it is still possible for the speaker to claim justifiably to have made a statement about just one of these individuals. For if it is the case that only one of these two individuals had several brothers and sisters, then the speaker can justifiably claim to have made a statement about that individual and, moreover, to have therefore made a true statement. That is, if the speaker uses a referring expression which applies to more than one individual, the speaker can truly claim to have made a statement about whichever individual has the predicated property. Of course, here a procedure for finding out which individual the speaker was talking about is identical with a procedure for finding out if the statement that he made is true. That is to say, a procedure for finding out which statement, in our sense of 'statement', the speaker made is in this case identical with a procedure for finding out if the statement which he made is true. For in each case what one can do is find out which of a given class of individuals has the predicated property (in this case, the property of having several brothers and sisters). It is, of course, possible to find out whether the speaker made a true statement without also thereby finding out which statement he made (that is, which individual his statement is about). For it is possible to find out that the individual whom his statement is about has the required property without also coming to know which individual he is. Nevertheless, in this kind of case there *is* a way of coming to know which statement the speaker made which is also *a* way of coming to know whether or not the statement that he made is true. And so if the speaker could use the

[1] A very similar sort of objection could be raised to the first case too.

predicate property to justify a claim about which individual his statement is about, this sort of case would be quite different from typical cases of statements. For in typical cases of statements, there is no procedure for either finding out which statement the speaker made or finding out whether his statement is true, which is also a procedure of doing the other. Normally, the predicate property is not used to determine which statement the speaker made.

But this is by no means to say that the predicate property cannot be used, in at least cases such as those described under (2) above, to determine which statement a speaker made. Whether or not this is ever possible will be considered in Section 7 of Chapter VII. It is clear that if the predicate property can be so used in at least some cases, then either (i) the predicate property can be so used because the predicate property is itself mentioned in the speaker's intention description or (ii) the predicate property can be so used just because it is the predicate property regardless of whether or not the predicate property is mentioned in the intention description. Second, it cannot be said that the predicate property is mentioned in the intention description just in virtue of being the predicate property because every property which the speaker believes to belong to the individual to whom he is trying to refer is thereby mentioned in the complete expression of the intention description. For it is not true that every property which the speaker believes to belong to that individual is thereby mentioned in the intention description. We saw in Section 5 that the used expression may mention a property which is not mentioned in the intention description even when the speaker believes that this property does belong to the individual in question. Suppose that this property is $\emptyset$; upon finding that, for example, no one has property $\emptyset$, the speaker can still say that he was trying to refer to a certain particular individual whom he can pick out from all others on the basis of the intention description. He can say that he was trying to refer to the individual who is U and Θ and that he thought that that individual was also $\emptyset$ but was wrong about this. As we also saw, $\emptyset$ is not necessarily mentioned in the intention description even if the intention description has the form 'the individual who has a sufficient number of . . .'. Third, if the predicate property is necessarily mentioned in the intention description, then there can be no cases of non-selective referring except those which are made by uttering analytic sentences or sentences in the referring expression of which is mentioned the predicate property. For since the predicate property is, by hypothesis, necessarily mentioned in the intention description, the used expression can constitute the intention description only if the predicate property is mentioned in the used expression as well. Only then will the intention description not "go beyond" the intention description.[1]

15 *Changes in the speaker's intention description*

Let us suppose that the speaker uses the name 'Nelson' to make a statement about an individual and, when asked about whom he is talking, the speaker says "I am talking about the man who is mayor of this city, who lives in that house over there, and who is now running for U.S. Representative from this district". Suppose the speaker is then told that the man who is mayor and is running for the House of Representatives from this district lives in another part of town. The speaker then replies "Well, I'm talking about the mayor who is running for the House of Representatives; perhaps I was mistaken about where he lives". The speaker's reply might not indicate that his intention with respect to his statement is now different from what his intention was when he made that statement. For his original intention might, as we have seen previously, have the form 'the individual who has a sufficient number of ...'. And it might be sufficient for an individual to have the properties of being mayor and being a candidate for the House of Representatives in order that that individual be the one about whom the speaker is trying to make a statement.

But this kind of reply might instead indicate a change in the speaker's intention description. Consider the following case. The speaker's intention description mentions the properties of being mayor, being named 'Nelson', being a candidate, and living in that house over there. Also, in fact the mayor is named 'Nelson' and the man running for the House from this district (and who is not the mayor) lives in that house. Here two different individuals each have a sufficient number of properties, since having two of

[1] The question of whether the predicate property can be mentioned in the intention description will be discussed in Section 7 of Chapter VII.

these properties was sufficient in the previous case. But now suppose that the speaker says "I am referring to the one who is mayor". If the speaker says this, then perhaps not all of the properties mentioned in the intention description are of the same importance and his intention description does not merely have the form 'the individual who has a sufficient number of . . .'. The property of being mayor is more important than the others since this property can indicate which of the two individuals it is to whom the speaker is referring.

But a second possibility is this. It is possible that in replying "I am referring to the mayor", the speaker is not indicating that the property of being mayor is more important in this way than the other properties mentioned in the intention description. Instead, what the speaker may be doing is indicating that his intention description has changed. He may be indicating that the following has taken place: when the speaker uttered the sentence in question, he intended thereby to make a statement about the individual who is mayor, is named 'Nelson', is running for the House of Representatives, and lives in this house, without regarding any of these properties as more important than the others in so far as what he intends in uttering that sentence is concerned; that is, he does not intend, at the time of uttering this sentence, that if no individual has all of these properties, then his statement is to be about, say, the one who is mayor; but upon finding that no individual has all of these properties, he then forms the intention that the sentence which he uttered be taken to be the making of a statement which is about the mayor; this is a different intention from that which he had previously, and one which involves a different intention description—'the individual who is mayor' rather than 'the individual who is mayor, is named "Nelson", is running for the House, and lives in this house'. If this is what has happened in a given case, then it is the new intention description which comes to govern the uttered sentence. The speaker did not succeed in making a statement at the time at which he uttered the sentence because his intention description did not apply to just one individual. But after his intention description changes in the above way—or, to put this in a better way, after he comes to have the new intention description 'the individual who is mayor'—it becomes true that he has then made a statement which is about just one individual. The statement which he has made is the statement which one makes by uttering the sentence in association with the speaker's new intention description. Let us suppose that the sentence was originally uttered at time t_1 and that the speaker comes to have his new intention description at time t_2 (where t_2 is later than t_1). Then at t_1 the speaker did not make a statement since what he said was not about a particular individual in view of his intention description at t_1. But we may say that the speaker does make (at t_2) a statement which is about a particular individual at t_2 even though he does not utter that sentence again at t_2. By coming to have at t_2 a new intention which is associated with the utterance of that sentence at t_1 (although this intention is not the intention with which he uttered that sentence at t_1), the speaker makes a statement at t_2. He does this by saying 'I am referring to the one who is mayor'. Thus, at a given time t_2 a speaker can make the statement which can be made by uttering a certain sentence with a certain intention and yet without uttering that sentence at t_2 if that sentence was uttered earlier than t_2 in the kind of circumstances described above. The speaker does this by coming to have, and indicating that he has come to have, the intention in question (or an intention similar to the one in question).

Whether a given case is a case of this sort or instead a case in which the intention description is of the form 'the individual who has a sufficient number of . . . ' or possibly a case in which one of the properties mentioned in the intention description is more important than the others can be determined by finding out whom the speaker would consider himself to have made a statement about in a variety of possible situations.

VII

THE INTENTION–DESCRIPTION
THEORY OF REFERRING
II

1 *Introduction*

In this chapter I wish to discuss certain objections that might be raised to the Intention–Description Theory of Referring and various topics which are related to these objections.

2 *Necessary and sufficient conditions of a name's denoting an individual*

In Section 6 of Chapter VI, I said that on the Intention–Description Theory of Referring, proper names do not have meanings. It might still be said—and would probably be said by, for example, Sørensen—that it follows from the Intention–Description Theory of Referring that proper names do have meanings. Sørensen says that to know the meaning of a "sign" is to know the necessary and sufficient conditions of that sign's denoting an individual.[1] He explains his use of the term 'denotes' in this way: "The extra-linguistic entity or entities we refer to by means of a sign S, I call the *denotatum* or *denotata* of S".[2] Thus, Sørensen might say the following about the Intention–Description Theory of Referring: let us suppose that a speaker uses the name 'Briggs' in association with the intention description 'the individual who built the first aeroplane'. That is, the speaker is using 'Briggs' with the intention

[1] H. Steen Sørensen, *The Meaning of Proper Names* (Gad, Copenhagen, 1963), pp. 39, 92.
[2] Sørensen, p. 14.

132

of referring to the individual who built the first aeroplane. Thus, the necessary and sufficient conditions of this token of 'Briggs' "denoting" a certain individual are that the individual be named 'Briggs',[1] that the individual be an individual to have built the first aeroplane, and that he be the only such individual. Therefore, on Sørensen's theory of meaning—the meaning of a sign being the necessary and sufficient conditions of the sign's denoting a certain individual—the meaning of this token of 'Briggs' is "the one and only individual who is named 'Briggs' and who built the first aeroplane". So this token of the name 'Briggs' does have a descriptive meaning.

However, this objection is not sound. For there is no single set of conditions which are necessary and sufficient for a speaker to refer to a particular individual by using a name. Let us suppose, as above, that the speaker uses 'Briggs' in association with the intention description 'the individual who built the first aeroplane' (where, as above, to say that a name is used in association with a certain intention description is only to say that the name is used on that occasion with the intention of referring to the one and only individual who built the first aeroplane). If there is more than one individual named 'Briggs', then it is sufficient for the speaker to have referred to—that is, made a statement which is about—an individual that that individual be the one and only individual who built the first aeroplane and be named 'Briggs'. But if there is only one individual named 'Briggs', then it is sufficient for this that that individual be the one and only individual named 'Briggs'. If there is only one individual named 'Briggs', then if the speaker utters the sentence 'Briggs was born in 1843', the speaker has made a statement about that individual whether or not that individual satisfies the associated intention description. If there was only one individual named 'Andrew Jackson', then if a speaker says "Andrew Jackson was elected President of the United States in 1964", he has made a statement about a certain former President of the United States and, moreover, a statement which is false. For if the speaker denies that he made a statement about that former President, it can be truly replied to him that "that is what he said" even if it is not what he meant to say (see Section 2 of Chapter

[1] As we saw in Section 2 of Chapter VI, it is necessary that the individual be named 'Briggs' in order that the speaker succeed in referring to him by using 'Briggs'.

VI). So there are at least two sufficient conditions of the speaker's making a statement which is about a certain individual by using this token of 'Briggs'. Consequently, neither of these conditions is a necessary condition of the speaker's making a statement which is about an individual by using this token of 'Briggs'. Consequently, there is no set of conditions which alone or together are *both* necessary and sufficient for the speaker's doing this. Hence, this token of 'Briggs' has no meaning on Sørensen's position.

It might be replied here that what is meant by 'necessary and sufficient conditions' is "conditions which are necessary and sufficient *in a particular set of circumstances*". Thus, if several individuals have the name 'Briggs', then it is not sufficient *in this situation* for the speaker to have made a statement about a particular individual that that individual have the name 'Briggs'. So in this situation it is not only sufficient but may also be necessary that the individual be the only individual named 'Briggs' and be a builder of the first aeroplane. Hence, *in this situation* the meaning of the used token of 'Briggs' is "the one and only individual named 'Briggs' who built the first aeroplane".

It appears that what is being said here is this: the name-token has a meaning when the speaker does succeed in referring to a certain particular individual. And its meaning is the meaning of that description which mentions the set of properties in virtue of having which that individual is the one whom the speaker's statement is about. For example, in the preceding paragraph, the speaker made a statement about the individual in question because that individual was the only individual *in that* situation who had the properties of being named 'Briggs' and being a builder of the first aeroplane. But this reply is not satisfactory either. For there can be situations in which the speaker does make a statement which is about a particular individual and yet there is no set of properties which either alone or together it is *both* necessary and sufficient that the individual have in that situation in order that that individual be the one whom the speaker's statement is about. Consider the following situation: there is only one individual named 'Briggs' and that individual was a builder of the first aeroplane. In this situation there are two distinct sets of properties which are sufficient for an individual's being the one whom the speaker's statement is about: (i) being the one and only individual named 'Briggs'; (ii) being named 'Briggs' and being a builder of the first aeroplane. The speaker does make a statement about the individual in question, but it is not clear in virtue of which of these two sets of properties the speaker does so. To put this in another way, in this situation neither (i) nor (ii) consists of properties the having of which by an individual are necessary for that individual's being the one whom the speaker's statement is about, since each of (i) and (ii) constitutes a sufficient condition of this. So it is not clear that in this case the name-token has one or the other meaning here. That is, it is not clear whether, on the view being discussed, the meaning of this token of 'Briggs' is "the one and only individual named 'Briggs' " or instead "the one and only individual who both is named 'Briggs' and is a builder of the first aeroplane". It seems that Sørensen would have to say that neither of these is the meaning of this token, since he talks about necessary conditions in stating what the meaning of a name-token is. Hence, it is plausible to say that on this view, this name-token has no meaning. Yet it is also true that on this view this name-token must have a meaning. For this view, like all versions of the Abbreviation Theory of Referring, maintains that it is in virtue of the meaning of a name-token that the speaker succeeds in referring to a particular individual. And the speaker in the above case has succeeded in referring to a particular individual by using this token of 'Briggs'.

Second, the principle on which this view is based seems to be false. It is not true that an expression which "denotes" an individual has the same meaning as the description which sets forth the necessary and sufficient conditions of being the individual "denoted" by that expression. Let us suppose that the description 'the U.S. Senator' is used in association with the intention description 'the senior U.S. Senator from New York'. Yet this token of 'the U.S. Senator' certainly does not have the same *meaning* as the description 'the senior U.S. Senator from New York', even if the latter does set forth a necessary and sufficient condition of being the individual denoted by the former. It cannot be replied that the principle in question applies only to names. For this view holds that names have descriptive meaning. And so any principle which tells under what conditions names have descriptive meaning should also apply in a similar way to other types of expressions which have the same type of descriptive meaning that names are alleged to have. After all, names and descriptions are very similar to one another in being "denoting" expressions and in having descriptive meaning, according to this view. Since the principle on which this view is based is false, that view gives no reason to say that proper names or their tokens have descriptive meaning.

3 The speaker's referring but not in virtue of his intention description

Another objection that might be raised to the Intention–Description Theory of Referring is this. Suppose that a speaker says "The Worchester Hotel has 1560 rooms". The hearer does not believe that there is any hotel called 'the Worchester Hotel' but wishes the speaker to continue to believe that there is such a hotel and so says "Yes, the Worchester Hotel is quite large". Let us now suppose that there is not only one hotel by this name but several hotels having this name and that the speaker (the one who made the first statement) has made a statement about one of these hotels in virtue of using the name 'the Worchester Hotel' in association with a certain intention description. We would then say that the hearer has, in this situation, not only made a statement which is about a hotel but also one which is about exactly the same hotel that the speaker's statement is about. Yet, since the hearer did not believe that there is any such hotel, he certainly did not intend to refer to such a hotel by using the name 'the Worchester Hotel' and consequently did not succeed in doing so in virtue of an intention description which was associated with the token of the name that he uttered. So it is not true as previously claimed, that in a case in which more than one individual has the uttered name, it is necessary that the uttered token be associated with an intention description which applies to only one individual in order for the speaker to succeed in making a statement about a particular individual.

This case does not show that there need be no intention description involved in such a situation. Instead, at most what it shows is that the intention description in virtue of which a person succeeds in referring to a particular individual need not be an intention description which would be used in expressing *that* person's intention. The hearer in the above case did make a statement about that hotel in virtue of the *speaker's* intention description. The hearer's statement was about that hotel because the speaker's statement (that is, the first statement) is about that hotel. Thus, while it is typically the case that it is the intention description of the one who utters the token that makes the resulting statement a statement about a particular individual, it is possible for this to take place as the result of someone else having a certain intention description. It should be noticed, however, that not only is *an* intention description involved in the above case but also a statement (namely, the first statement) is made in the above case which is about a particular individual in virtue of the intention description *of the one who made that statement.*

4 *Referring to two different individuals by the use of one token*

It might be objected that the Intention–Description Theory of Referring allows a speaker to use a single token of a name or a description to refer successfully to more than one individual. If the token is used in association with two intention descriptions that are not only different descriptions but also uniquely characterize two different individuals, then it seems that the proponent of the Intention–Description Theory of Referring would have to say that this speaker has successfully referred to and made statements about those two individuals by using a single token. Thus, for example, the speaker could say "Cranston takes both civil and criminal cases" and thereby with one utterance make statements about two different individuals—that is, attribute the property of taking both civil and criminal cases to two different individuals.

Let us suppose that this is allowed by the Intention–Description Theory of Referring. That the theory allows this does not seem to be an objection to the theory. For it may be the case that a speaker *can* in fact use the utterance of a single sentence to make two different statements. To take a case similar to that described above, suppose the speaker uses the ambiguous sentence 'The gauge moved'. The hearer may ask "Did you say that the gauge indicated a different number from that which it previously indicated?", and the speaker can truly reply that this is what he said. The hearer can then ask "Did you say that the gauge moved from its resting place on the table?" and the speaker can also truly say that he said this too. There seems to be no reason why the speaker cannot make two statements at once by using an ambiguous sentence. Perhaps he may use one utterance of this sentence to make two different statements at the same time, each statement to a different hearer. The same thing could also perhaps be done by uttering a sentence which has both a meaning in a natural language and a code meaning. There are two hearers, one of whom does not know the code and the other of whom does not know the natural language in question. It seems to be possible for the speaker to utter this sentence with the intention of making both statements and being willing to regard part of what he said as false if either of these statements is false. Hence there seems to be no reason why a speaker cannot make two statements, each one about a different individual, by uttering one sentence which contains a name that is a name of each of these two individuals.

5 *Picking out or recognizing the individual whom the statement is about*

I have claimed that it is a necessary condition of a speaker's succeeding in referring to a particular individual that the speaker be able to give some description which applies uniquely to that individual. (The speaker can make a statement which is about an individual without satisfying this condition, if the used expression applies uniquely to that individual; but in such cases the speaker has not *succeeded* in referring to that individual because the speaker was not *trying* to refer to *that* individual if this condition is not satisfied.) The description which the speaker is able to give is part or all of this intention description (although he is perhaps able to give other descriptions too in some cases). It might be objected that a speaker can succeed in referring to an individual without being able to give a description of that individual. Ayer seems to be making this objection when he says it is not "a necessary condition of the significant use or understanding of a proper name that one should be able to furnish some description of the individual to whom the name refers".[1] (Presumably, what Ayer means here

[1] A. J. Ayer, 'Names and Descriptions', *The Concept of a Person* (Macmillan, London, 1964), p. 145.

by "to whom the name refers" is "to whom the speaker is using a token of that name to refer"). Ayer says that the speaker has referred successfully if the speaker can pick out or recognize that individual even if the speaker cannot give a description of that individual. Thus, Ayer does grant that the basis for saying in some cases that the speaker has referred to one individual rather than another is "up to the speaker"—it is the individual whom the speaker would pick out. But he claims that this basis can consist in the speaker's being able to recognize the individual rather than his being able to give a description of the individual.

However, it can be replied that in such cases—cases of recognition—the speaker can still say whom it is that he is talking about by using a descriptive phrase which expresses the speaker's intention description. In such cases, the intention description is 'the individual whom I would point to or otherwise pick out if I were asked to whom I was referring'. It might then be asked how it is determined that the individual whom the speaker does pick out in a given case of this sort is the individual to whom the speaker was in fact trying to refer. How is it determined that the speaker has in fact picked out the correct individual? The answer is that this is determined in the same way in which it is determined that a speaker in fact meant what he claims to have meant by an earlier utterance. After he uses the referring expression, the speaker may make a mistake by picking out an individual who is not the individual whom he would have picked out at the time he used the referring expression. The individual to whom he is referring is the individual whom he would pick out at the time he used the referring expression, just as in other cases the individual to whom he is referring is the individual who uniquely satisfies the intention description at the time he uses the referring expression.

6 Is the speaker referring to whomever his statements are uniquely true of?

I have said that a speaker succeeds in referring to an individual, in the sense of the term 'refer' in which the speaker's statement is about that individual only if the used referring expression applies to that individual (Section 2 of Chapter VI). That is, the applicability of the used expression to an individual is a necessary condition of the speaker's successfully referring to that individual. Several objections to this thesis were discussed at the end of Section 2 of Chapter VI. In this section I wish to discuss another possible objection to this thesis.

In the cases discussed in Chapter VI, what allegedly made the speaker's statement a statement about an individual who did not have the used name was, for example, that the speaker did use what is in fact a name of that individual both before and after the statement in question in the same conversation. Ayer suggests a different way of rendering the speaker's statement a statement about an individual to whom the used expression does not apply. He claims that a speaker succeeds in referring to whomever his statements are uniquely true of. He says "But so long as a particular individual is clearly identified by the statements that are made, identified in the sense that they are true of him and him only, then we say that this is the individual that is being referred to, no matter what name is used".[1]

This is in fact an objection to two different theses which I have maintained. First, as said earlier, it is an objection to the thesis that in order for a speaker to make a statement which is about a particular individual, it is necessary that the used expression apply to that individual. For this is not necessary if it is true that one or more statements can be about an individual of whom they are uniquely true even if the used expression does not apply to that individual. Second, this is also an objection to my thesis that if an individual is the one and only individual to whom the used expression applies, then any statement made by using that expression is about that individual, regardless of who, if anyone, uniquely satisfies the intention description of the speaker; that individual's being the one to whom the used expression uniquely applies is a sufficient indication of the statement's being about that individual. But if what Ayer says is true, then this is not a sufficient condition of the statement's being about this individual. For Ayer holds that if the property mentioned in the predicate of the statement belongs uniquely to an individual, then that statement is about that individual, regardless of whether or not some individual is one to whom the used expression uniquely applies. If Ayer is correct, the statement is about the individual who uniquely has the predicate

[1] Ayer (*op. cit.*), p. 141.

property rather than an individual to whom the used expression uniquely applies.

However, Ayer's position does not seem to be correct. If a speaker says "John F. Kennedy is the present British Prime Minister" or "John F. Kennedy is the 32nd President of the United States", we would not necessarily say that the speaker had referred to Harold Wilson or, in the second case, to Franklin D. Roosevelt, even though Harold Wilson uniquely has the property of being the present British Prime Minister and Roosevelt uniquely has the property of being the 32nd President of the United States. That we would not necessarily say that the speaker had referred to these individuals is shown by the fact that we would not necessarily say that what the speaker said was true or that the speaker's statements were true. For example, we might say to the speaker "No, it is not true that John F. Kennedy is the 32nd President; he is the 35th President, while Franklin D. Roosevelt was the 32nd President" and "No, John F. Kennedy is not the British Prime Minister; Harold Wilson is the British Prime Minister". This shows that the speaker's statements are not about Harold Wilson and Franklin D. Roosevelt. For if they were about these individuals, these statements would have been true. Thus, the speaker has not referred to these individuals in the sense of 'refer' in which it means "made a statement which is about". Thus, it is not true that a speaker refers to whatever individual his statement or statements are uniquely true of, regardless of what referring expression is used in making the statement.

Ayer's position also seems to be incorrect for the following reasons. First, let us suppose that the properties $\emptyset$ and Θ are properties that only Franklin D. Roosevelt had and that when the speaker is asked "Who had $\emptyset$ and Θ?" he replies "Woodrow Wilson had $\emptyset$ and Θ". Ayer would have to say that what the speaker says here is true even though it is false that Woodrow Wilson had $\emptyset$ and Θ. For since Roosevelt is the only one to have $\emptyset$ and Θ, Ayer must say that what the speaker said is about Roosevelt and is therefore true even though the speaker used a name—'Woodrow Wilson'—which is not one of Roosevelt's names. But in fact what the speaker said is false. Hence it is not true that a statement is about whoever it is to whom its predicate property uniquely applies.

Second, suppose that the speaker makes a statement by uttering a sentence of the form 'The individual who has property a has properties b, c, h, and n'. Suppose, further, that it is not the individual who has a that has b, c, h, and n but another individual who alone has all of these. Suppose, moreover, that the individual who has a also has b and c. The position being discussed would presumably have to say that the speaker referred to the individual who has all of these properties—for the group of predicated properties belongs only to that individual—while in fact we would say that he had referred to the individual who had a.

It might be replied that it is true that in, for example, the above cases in which the name 'John F. Kennedy' was used, we would not say that the speaker's statements were about Harold Wilson and Franklin D. Roosevelt. But this does not show that the position being discussed is wrong, for the cases are not the sorts of cases that it is to be applied to. In the quotation from Ayer, he talks about "statements" whereas in the cases discussed above, the speaker made only one statement in each case. Even if this position is not true of individual statements taken alone, this position may be true of cases in which the speaker makes *several* statements the predicate of *each* of which applies uniquely to one individual, or cases in which the speaker made several statements the predicate properties of which *as a group* applies to only one individual. For example, if a speaker made several statements by using the name 'Woodrow Wilson' but the predicate properties of which applied only to Roosevelt, it may be the case that these statements are about Roosevelt. It might also be claimed that in the case of a single statement in which *many* properties are predicated of an individual, that statement would be about the individual who alone had all of those properties regardless of what referring expression was used, whereas this might not be the case with a single statement in which only one property was predicated of an individual.

But even in cases of several statements or of a single statement in which many properties are predicated of an individual, it does not seem that the speaker is referring to whoever uniquely has these properties regardless of the referring expression used. Let us consider as an example a case in which the speaker makes several statements by using the name 'William Graham Sumner' but where the predicate properties each belong only to Charles Horton Cooley. In such a case it seems that we would say, not that these statements are about Cooley but instead either (1) that the speaker believes that Sumner is identical with Cooley, or (2) that the speaker believes that 'William Graham Sumner' is one of Cooley's names. It does not follow from either (1) or (2) that the speaker's statements are about Cooley. And in fact the speaker's statements are not about Cooley. For if the hearer were to ask "Are you saying that the sociologist who first used the term 'primary group' has those properties?" we would not say that the speaker could truly say "That's what I said".

Thus, the position being discussed does not seem to be true for any type of case if 'refers' is taken to mean "makes a statement which is in fact about". But, as pointed out in Section 10 of Chapter VI, there are two senses of 'refer'. And perhaps this position is true for the second sense of 'refer'—the sense in which to refer to an individual is to *try* to make a statement about that individual. The position, as applied to this sense of 'refer', is this: if the speaker makes a statement the predicate properties of which belong uniquely (at least together if not singly) to one individual, then the speaker is *trying* to make a statement about that individual, regardless of what referring expression the speaker uses in making this statement. This version of Ayer's thesis may well be true, as we will see in a moment. First, however, his view seems to be subject to the following objections. A speaker can use the name 'George Meredith' in an attempt to make a statement about someone who is neither George Meredith nor Thomas Hardy even though the properties mentioned in the statement belong exclusively to Thomas Hardy. For example, the speaker may say "George Meredith had his first great popular success with *Far from the Madding Crowd* in 1874". When asked about whom he is talking, the speaker may reply "I'm talking about the author of *Daniel Deronda*". In this case the speaker was trying to make a statement about George Eliot even though the predicate property belongs exclusively to Thomas Hardy.

One reason why it may seem that in cases in which there are several predicate properties each of which belong exclusively to one individual, the speaker is trying to refer to that individual, is this: It may seem that since the speaker believes that these predicate properties each belong to one particular individual, these properties are mentioned in the speaker's intention description and hence make that intention description one which is satisfied exclusively by the individual to which these predicate properties exclusively belong. But even if it is the case that the predicate properties of a statement are, either contingently or necessarily, mentioned in the speaker's intention description, it is still possible that the speaker's intention description is of the form 'the individual who has a sufficient number of . . . ' and that the predicate properties are outweighed by the other properties mentioned in the intention description. In such a case, this intention description is uniquely satisfied by an individual other than the one to whom the predicate properties uniquely belong.

Perhaps a more important reason why Ayer's thesis seems to be true for this second sense of 'refers' is this. When a speaker utters a sentence in order to make a subject-predicate statement, he is trying to make a statement which is about the individual, if any, to whom the predicate property belongs. If the predicate property belongs to more than one individual, then he is trying to make a statement about one of the individuals to whom the predicate property belongs. Let us suppose that James Clerk Maxwell is the individual to whom the predicate property exclusively belongs. Perhaps it is then true to say that if the speaker is trying to make a statement about the individual to whom the predicate property exclusively belongs, and Maxwell is that individual, then the speaker is trying to make a statement about Maxwell. If this is true, then Ayer's thesis is true for the second sense of 'refers'. For Ayer's thesis as applied to this second sense of 'refers' is that the speaker is trying to make a statement about Maxwell if Maxwell is the individual to whom the predicate property exclusively belongs.

But even if the speaker is trying to make a statement about Maxwell in this sort of case, it is also true that this is not necessarily the only thing which the speaker is trying to do in uttering this sentence. The speaker is, generally, also trying to make a statement about the individual who uniquely satisfies his intention description. If that individual is Henri Poincaré, then the speaker is trying to make a statement about Poincaré. Therefore, at one and the same time by the use of one and the same sentence, the speaker can be trying to make a statement about Poincaré and trying to make a statement about Maxwell. Moreover, it is always the intention description and never the predicate properties which determines which individual his statement *is in fact about*, although both the intention description and the predicate properties may determine which individual or individuals the speaker is *trying* to make a statement about. Thus, Ayer's thesis may be true for the second sense of 'refers', although not the first sense of 'refers', if it is possible for a speaker to be trying to make a statement about two different individuals at one time when the referring expression is of the sort that can pick out only one individual at a time.

7 *Predicate properties and intention descriptions*

In Section 14 of Chapter VI and at the end of Section 6 of this chapter, the question of whether the predicate property of a statement can be, is always, or is necessarily, mentioned in the speaker's intention description was raised and discussed to some extent. There seems to be no reason why in at least some cases the predicate property cannot be mentioned in the speaker's intention description. To take an example, there seems to be no reason why, in making the statement "Wiggins knows Aramaic", the speaker cannot express his intention in using 'Wiggins' partly by mentioning the property of knowing Aramaic. This is clearly possible in cases in which the intention description is of the form 'the individual who has a sufficient number of . . . '. For in these cases, it is clearly possible for the speaker to succeed in referring to an individual and for his statement to be false. The main objection to holding that the predicate property is mentioned in the intention description is this: if the predicate property were mentioned in the intention description, then the predicate property would play a role in rendering the statement a statement about a certain particular individual; and then there could be no false statements; for then if an individual does not have the predicate property, then that individual is not the one whom the statement is about; hence there cannot be a statement which is about an individual and is false—that is, where that individual does not have the predicate property—if the predicate property is mentioned in the intention description; the statement will be about that individual only if that individual has the predicate property, that is, only if that statement is true; but since any statement can be either true or false, no predicate property can be mentioned in the speaker's intention description. As noted earlier, this objection does not apply to cases in which the speaker's intention description is of the form 'the individual who has a sufficient number of . . . '. For such an intention description can be uniquely satisfied by an individual who does not have one or even several of the properties mentioned in that intention description: an individual can have a sufficient number of the properties mentioned in the intention description without having all of them. Consequently, the above objection does not show that the predicate property cannot be mentioned in intention descriptions of the form 'the individual who has a sufficient number of . . . '.

But can this also be so in a case of the following sort: the speaker says "John is my uncle's brother-in-law" and the intention description mentions the property of being the present governor of New York State? Could this intention description also mention only one other property—that of being my uncle's brother-in-law—so that the intention description is 'the individual who is the present governor of New York State and is my uncle's brother-in-law'? Even in such cases, it may be said, the predicate property could be mentioned in the intention description and yet the statement could be false, for the other mentioned property (in this case being governor of New York State) could be regarded by the speaker as being more important than the predicate property. The former is more important than the latter in at least some of the cases in which the speaker would also say that if no individual named 'John' had both of these properties, then his statement is about the one who has the former property only. But if the speaker were to say this, what reason would there be to say that the latter (in this case, the predicate) property was mentioned in his intention description at all? Why shouldn't we say that he is trying to refer to the governor of New York State regardless of the governor's family relationships? Hence this does not seem to be a way of allowing the predicate property to be mentioned in the intention description and yet for the statement to be possibly false.

Let us now suppose that the predicate property is in fact mentioned in the intention description—that is, that the intention description is 'the individual who is governor of New York State and is my uncle's brother-in-law' and that the speaker would say that he does not know to whom he was referring if in fact no individual has *both* of the properties mentioned here in the intention description (this latter being the test of a property's being mentioned in an intention description which is *not* of the form 'the individual who has a sufficient number of . . . '). In such a case, if the speaker succeeds in making a statement at all of the sort which he wants to make, namely one about an individual who uniquely satisfies the intention description, that statement will be a true statement. For he succeeds in making a statement at all of the sort which he wants to make only by succeeding in referring to someone who has the predicate property. So in this case it is true that the speaker cannot succeed in making a false statement of the sort which he wants to make. But it does not follow from this that he cannot make a false statement in this case by uttering the sentence in question in association with the intention description in question. For it is possible that there is one and only one individual who bears the name 'John'[1] and that that individual is not 'my uncle's brother-in-law'. Then the speaker would make *a* statement (about that individual) and one which was false. So if it must be possible in every case in which a speaker uses a sentence containing a referring expression as its subject for the speaker to make *a* false statement, then this requirement is satisfied even if the predicate property is mentioned in this sort of intention description. Of course, in such cases the speaker may not be able to make a false statement of the sort which he wants to make. But it is not clear that in every case it must be possible for the speaker to make a false statement *of the sort of statement which he wants to make*. It may only be necessary that it be possible for the speaker to make *a* false statement in every such case.

Thus, there seems to be no reason to say that the predicate property cannot be mentioned in the intention description in every case. And there is a strong reason for saying that the predicate property is mentioned in the intention description in every case, namely that by saying this, we can explain what it is for the speaker to intend to make a statement about the (or an) individual

[1] It will be remembered that the sentence which the speaker utters is 'John is my uncle's brother-in-law'.

having the predicate property. What it is for the speaker to do this is for the speaker to use the uttered expression with the intention of referring to an individual who has the predicate property. That is, the predicate property figures in his intention description so that what it is for him to intend to make a statement about an individual who has the predicate property is exactly the same as what it is for him to intend to make a statement about an individual who has some property mentioned in the intention description other than the predicate property. Of course, it is still possible to regard the speaker's intention to refer to an individual who is governor of New York State as a different intention from the speaker's intention to refer to an individual who is his uncle's brother-in-law even though both of the properties "being governor of New York State" and "being my uncle's brother-in-law" are mentioned in the speaker's intention description. But this can be said of any two properties mentioned in the intention description.

I claim that it is possible for the predicate property to be mentioned in intention descriptions, even those not of the form 'the individual who has a sufficient number of . . . '. However, it is not necessary for the predicate property to be mentioned in the intention description. For a speaker could make a statement which he believes to be false. In such a case he is not trying to make a statement about an individual who has the predicate property. Hence in such a case there is no reason to say that the predicate property is mentioned in the speaker's intention description and a strong reason to say that the predicate property is not so mentioned.

It follows from the view which I have been defending that if the speaker says "Briggs played the violin" in association with the intention description 'the builder of the first aeroplane who was named "Briggs" ' and finds that there were two individuals named 'Briggs' involved in the building of the first aeroplane, the speaker can correctly say that he made a statement which is about the one who played the violin and therefore made a true statement. It could not be truly denied that that was the individual about whom he was talking and that what he said was true. This follows from the view which I am defending because I am defending the view that the predicate property can be used to identify both whom the speaker is talking about (in the sense of trying to make a statement about) and whom the speaker's statement is in fact about.

That the predicate property is mentioned in the intention description does not render the speaker's statement necessarily true, when the speaker succeeds in making a statement of the sort which he wants to make. First, on the Intention–Description Theory of Referring, the uttered referring expression does not have the same meaning as the intention description. Moreover, as we saw in discussing the Abbreviation Theory of Referring, the expressing of analytic sentences does not necessarily result in the making of statements that are necessary truths. So even if the referring expression did have the same meaning as the intention description, it does not follow from this that if the predicate property is mentioned in the intention description, the speaker thereby makes a statement which is necessarily true when he makes a true statement of the sort which he wants to make.

The following objection might be raised to the position which I am defending in this section. It might be said that every property which is mentioned in the intention description can be mentioned in answer to the question "To whom are you referring?" Let us suppose that the speaker says "The Senator is in Washington today" in association with the intention description 'the individual who is the senior United States Senator from New York . . . ' (the dots indicate that other properties are mentioned in this intention description too). If the speaker is asked to whom he is referring, the speaker can say, for example, "to the senior Senator from New York". For the purpose of replying to this question, he can mention any of the properties mentioned in his intention description. But one thing that he would not say is this: "I am referring to the Senator who is in Washington today". That is, the speaker would not mention the predicate property in trying to explain to whom he is referring. And since the speaker can mention any property mentioned in the intention description in trying to explain this, this shows that the predicate property is not mentioned in the intention description.

But this is not correct. The reason why the speaker would not mention the predicate property in explaining to whom he is referring is that the hearer already believes that the speaker believes that the individual to whom the speaker is referring has the predicate property. For the speaker mentioned the predicate property in making his statement. So it would not give further help in identification to the hearer if the hearer were told that this individual has the predicate property—the speaker has already said that he has that property. So this objection does not show that the predicate property is not mentioned in the intention description, since what properties the speaker mentions in explaining whom he is talking about depends partly on what the speaker believes about what the hearer already knows.

8 *The uttered expression's applying to the individual whom the statement is about*

Another objection to the claim that a necessary condition of a statement's being about an individual is that the uttered expression apply to that individual is this. There are some situations (besides those discussed towards the end of Section 2 of Chapter VI) in which the speaker can make a statement about a certain particular individual even though the uttered expression does not apply to that individual. The following is an example of such a situation: there is one and only one person in front of the speaker and in fact this person is, other than the hearer who is standing beside the speaker, the only person who is in the speaker's vicinity who can be seen from the place where the speaker and the hearer are standing; the speaker says "That man once met Frank Lloyd Wright" while pointing in the direction of the one and only person who is in front of him, or he says "The man in front of me once met Frank Lloyd Wright"; the person who is in front of the speaker is in fact a woman. Here the used expression—'that man' or 'the man in front of me'—does not apply to or, in the case of the latter expression, only partly applies to the person in front of the speaker, for this person is a woman. Yet, it might be claimed, the speaker's statement is certainly about that person even if that person is a woman. Hence, it is not a necessary condition of a statement's being about an individual that the used expression apply to that individual.

This case might well be a case of the speaker's trying to make a statement about the person in front of him. It is probably a case of the speaker's succeeding in referring the hearer to that indi-

THE INTENTION–DESCRIPTION THEORY OF REFERRING

vidual, and, if the person had met Frank Lloyd Wright, a case of the speaker's conveying information about the person to the hearer. But on what grounds can it be said to be a statement about that person? After all, it does not follow from the fact that everyone knows very well whom the speaker is trying to refer to, that the speaker has succeeded in referring to that person. The case being discussed is such that there can be no question about whom the speaker is trying to refer to. But we have already seen that there is a great difference between referring to an individual and referring a hearer to an individual (see Section 11 of Chapter VI) and that a speaker can, intentionally or unintentionally, refer a hearer to an individual without thereby referring to that individual. In the case being discussed, we know very well what statement (in our sense of the term 'statement') the speaker *meant* to make, but it does not follow from this that he *made* that statement. The hearer can reply to the speaker "That's not true", but here the hearer, if he knows that the person in front of the speaker is not a man, is saying that the statement which the speaker meant to make is not true, not that the statement which the speaker did make is not true.

In cases like this one, the speaker cannot truly say "That's what I said" when asked an appropriate question by the speaker, although he can truly say "That's what I meant" (see Section 2 of Chapter VI). Therefore, the speaker's statement was not about the person in front of him. If we do say that the speaker's statement is about that individual, then we must say that the speaker's intending to refer to a certain individual is a sufficient condition of his doing so, provided that that individual exists.[1] But if we do say this latter, then it seems that we must say that the speaker succeeds in referring to a particular individual even if the speaker utters an expression which has nothing whatsoever to do with the individual in question, as long as the speaker has the required

---

[1] That this is a sufficient condition of the speaker's statement being about a particular individual seems to be maintained by L. Linsky. For he says that a speaker can refer successfully to an individual as the husband of a certain lady even if that lady is a spinster ('Reference and Referents', in C. Caton (ed.), *Philosophy and Ordinary Language* (Illinois, 1963), p. 80). See also, on this topic, K. Donnellan, 'Reference and Definite Descriptions', *Philosophical Review*, LXXV (1966); and A. MacKay, 'Mr. Donnellan and Humpty Dumpty on Referring', and K. Donnellan, 'Putting Humpty Dumpty Together Again', both in *Philosophical Review*, LXXVII (1968).

intention. But this cannot be correct, as the cases in Section 2 of Chapter VI show.

It might be said that the speaker in the case described above does succeed in referring to that individual because not all of the properties mentioned by the speaker in uttering the used expression are equally important. For example, in the case in which 'the man in front of me' is the used expression, the property of being in front of the speaker is the important property while that of being a man is not the important one. However, this position of the objector does not seem to be correct either. For instead of a case in which the individual does have some of the mentioned properties, we could use a case in which the individual has none of the mentioned properties and yet it is just as clear whom it is that the speaker is trying to make a statement about. Even on the revised position of the objector, the speaker could not be said to have made a statement about this individual in this case. For there are no mentioned properties at all that the individual in question has here. Consequently, this revised type of objection to our position is not sound.

VIII

ABOUTNESS

---

1 *Reference and aboutness are different from one another*

In the previous five chapters, I have talked about referring—in particular, about the problem of ambiguous reference and the conditions of successful referring. Thus, I have been talking about a certain activity which people engage in. For it is speakers, rather than expressions or whole statements, which refer.[1] But, as I have indicated throughout this book, although statements do not refer, they do stand in a certain relation to individuals, namely the relation of being about particular individuals.[2] Reference is a relation between a speaker and an individual, while aboutness is a relation between a statement and an individual. But, of course, these two relations—reference and aboutness—are themselves related to one another. For it is by referring successfully to an individual that a speaker makes a statement which is about that individual. So in discussing the conditions of successful reference in previous chapters, we have been talking about the conditions of making a statement which is about a particular individual. But it is a separate question as to what it is for a statement to be about a particular individual. And it is this next question that I will take up in this chapter.

As a start towards answering the question "What is it for a statement to be about a particular individual?" I will first try to show that existence statements are not about particular individuals, at least not in the way in which subject–predicate statements are about individuals. My purpose in doing this is to specify a

[1] See L. Linsky, *Referring*, p. 116.
[2] At least, those statements of the type which we are mainly considering in this book, namely those made by using names and descriptive phrases, are about individuals.

condition of adequacy for any theory of aboutness which purports to explain the aboutness of subject–predicate statements. If existence statements are not about individuals in the way in question, then any such theory should explain aboutness in a way which brings out this fact about existence statements. In the last section of this chapter, I will suggest a theory of aboutness which seems quite plausible and which also meets this condition of adequacy.

One point must be emphasized before proceeding. I have said that reference and aboutness are two different things and that to explain one is not to explain the other. It might be objected that this is not so. The objector might hold that to explain one is to explain the other, and that in fact in discussing reference in the previous five chapters, I have said all that can be said and needs to be said about aboutness too. Several paragraphs ago I tried to establish that reference and aboutness were different by asserting that one is a relation between a speaker and an individual while the other is a relation between a statement and an individual. But, the objector might claim, the second relation can be reduced to the first in the following way: For a statement to be about an individual is for that statement to be made by a speaker who referred successfully to that individual in the course of making that statement.

Of course, this can go equally well in the other direction: For a speaker to refer successfully to an individual is for that speaker to make a statement which is about that individual.[1] Which way (if either way) should this go? My own view is that it should go in the second way. In the previous five chapters I have set forth the conditions of successful referring. But I have not said what successful referring is. I believe that to refer successfully to an individual is to make a statement which is about that individual. But to substantiate this, I must at the very least give some account of aboutness which does not mention referring. And that is what I will try to do in this chapter. Doing this will also refute the objector's claim that there is nothing more to be said about aboutness beyond what has been said in the previous five chapters.

---

[1] If we take it as going in this direction, we will also have to say such things as this: when a speaker says "Fleming went . . ." and is interrupted so that he does not finish making his statement, the speaker has only tried to refer and has not succeeded in referring to Fleming because he did not make a statement which is about Fleming.

This will not definitively settle the matter, of course. It is still possible that my own theory of aboutness, while admittedly describing a property which statements have, does not describe the property of aboutness but instead describes some other property. Nevertheless, I think that it has a good deal of plausibility as a theory of aboutness.

Moreover, the objector's proposed reduction of aboutness to referring may establish only a relation between referring and the *making* of a statement. The apparent plausibility of the proposed reduction may only show that if a statement is about an individual, then that statement can be *made* only by a speaker who refers successfully to that individual. And this is quite different from showing that successful referring to the individual is identical with the statement's being about the individual.

2 *Existence statements are not about particular individuals*

The reader will remember that I discussed existence statements and subject–predicate statements in Section 2 of Chapter II.[1] My purpose there was very different from my present purpose. My purpose there was to show that ostensible subject–predicate statements are not themselves existence statements. And I tried to show this by showing that there are situations in which a subject–predicate statement has a different truth-value from that of the correlative existence statement. But even if subject–predicate statements are not identical with existence statements, both could still be about particular individuals and, moreover, about particular individuals in the very same way. In this section I want to show that existence statements are not about individuals in the very same way, if indeed they are about individuals at all.

The term 'existence statement' will be used, as before, to mean "statements made by using sentences of the form 'There exists an

[1] The reader will also have noticed that I regard existence statements as being statements. And the question may arise as to whether existence statements are statements in my sense of the term 'statement'—the sense in which if two statements attribute the same property to the same individual, they are the same statement. The answer is "no". For, as I try to show in this section, existence statements are not about individuals and hence do not attribute properties to individuals. So when I call existence statements "statements", I am using the term 'statement' in a broader way, a way which includes both existence statements and subject–predicate statements.

individual (or one and only one individual) who has the properties . . . ' ' ". There are other types of statements to which the term
'existence statement' could justifiably be applied, for example,
statements made by using sentences of the form ' . . . exists' (where
the dots stand for a proper name). But these statements will not be
discussed in this chapter since these statements have a subject–
predicate grammatical form and may even be subject–predicate
statements. This is only to say that I will use the term 'existence
statement' only to mean "Statements made by using sentences of
the form 'There exists an individual (or one and only one individual) who has the properties . . . ' " because I wish to contrast
existence statements with subject–predicate statements.

Let us suppose that there are several individuals named 'Mills'
and that all of these individuals know Greek. In this situation the
statement "There is an individual named 'Mills' who knows
Greek" is true. Which of the individuals named 'Mills' is this
statement about? There is no reason to say that this statement is
about one of these individuals rather than another. There is no
way of telling which one of these individuals the statement is
about. There is no possible basis on which it could be justifiably
said that this statement is about one of these individuals rather
than another. Hence, this statement is not about a particular
individual.

One possible objection is this. It is true that there is no reason
to say that the existence statement is about one of these individuals
named 'Mills' rather than another. Nevertheless, this statement can
be regarded as *being* about *each* of these individuals. That is, the
statement is about each member of a certain group of individuals.
And this is compatible with the statement's not being about one
of these individuals *rather than* another.

But what group of individuals is it of which the statement is
about each member? There are at least three possible groups here:
(i) the exclusive disjunctive group—all those who are either
named 'Mills' or know Greek but not both; (ii) the inclusive
disjunctive group—all those who are either named 'Mills' or know
Greek or both; (iii) the conjunctive group—all and only those
who are both named 'Mills' and know Greek.

Let us consider the exclusive disjunctive group first. When a
subject–predicate statement is about an individual, then if that

statement is true, it is about the individual whose having of certain properties renders that statement true. But if the existence statement were true and were about the exclusive disjunctive group, the existence statement would not be about any individual whose existence renders that statement true. For it is the existence of an individual who has *both* the properties of being named 'Mills' and knowing Greek that renders this statement true. And no such individual belongs to the exclusive disjunctive group. So if the existence statement is about the members of the exclusive disjunctive group, it is about each of those members in a way different from that in which a subject–predicate statement is about a certain individual. This objection does not apply to (ii) and (iii) since the inclusive disjunctive group and the conjunctive group could contain an individual having both of these properties. But again, if the existence statement is about each of the members of the inclusive disjunctive group, it is about each of those individuals in a way different from that in which a subject–predicate statement is about an individual. For a subject–predicate statement is about *only* individuals whose properties are relevant to the statement's being true or false. But if the existence statement is about each of the members of the inclusive disjunctive group, then that statement can be about an individual—namely, one who is either named 'Mills' or knows Greek but not both—whose properties are not relevant to the truth or falsity of the statement. It is not in virtue of an individual's *only* being named 'Mills' or *only* knowing Greek that the statement is true, if it is true. So the statement could be about an individual whose having of certain properties have nothing whatever to do with the statement's being true, which is not the case with subject–predicate statements.

Now let us turn to the conjunctive group. A subject–predicate statement of the type in question is about an individual even when it is false. But an existence statement which is about each member of the conjunctive group is false if and only if it is not about any individual. For if the conjunctive group has a member, then the statement is true; but then *and only then* is the statement about an individual on alternative (iii). If the conjunctive group has no members (or does not exist), then the statement is false and about no one; for there is no member of the group for the statement to be about. Thus, the statement is, on alternative (iii), about an individual if and only if that statement is true. On alternative (iii) not only can the existence statement be false when the statement is not about any individual, but moreover that statement is false if and only if it is not about any individual.[1] But a subject–predicate statement can be about an individual even when it is false. "Jones is forty years old" can be about Jones even if he is fifty years old. So on alternative (iii) also, an existence statement is not about an individual in the way in which a subject–predicate statement is about an individual. These two types of statements differ greatly with respect to the relation between falsity and aboutness. Hence, on all of these alternatives, if there is a sense of 'about' in which an existence statement can be about an individual, it is a different sense from that in which a subject–predicate statement is about an individual. And what we are trying to determine in this chapter is what it is for a statement to be about an individual in the sense of 'about' in which a subject–predicate statement is about an individual.

It might now be said that existence statements can be about particular individuals because these statements can be associated with the speaker's intentions in the same way in which subject–predicate statements can. For example, in making the statement "There exist men who play the bassoon", the speaker may intend thereby to refer to and make a statement about George. It is possible that the speaker may have such an intention in making this statement. But that the speaker has this intention does not show that he succeeds in carrying it out. Thus, that the speaker has this intention does not show that his existence statement either is or can be about George. It might then be said that what shows that this existence statement can *be* about an individual is that the individual in question can be *mentioned* in the making of the statement. Thus, the speaker may say "There exist men, namely George, who play the bassoon". But even this does not show that this existence statement is about George in the required way. For this statement seems to be a conjunction of two statements:

[1] It is also the case that on alternatives (i) and (ii) an existence statement could be false without being about any individual; for the statement can be false while the inclusive disjunctive and the exclusive disjunctive groups have no members. And this is another reason for saying that on alternatives (i) and (ii) the existence statement is not about an individual in the way in which a subject–predicate statement is about an individual.

"There exist men who play the bassoon and George is a man who plays the bassoon". It is true that this *conjunction* is about George in the required way. That this conjunction is about George is shown by (*a*) the fact that a hearer can appropriately ask "Which George do you mean?" and (*b*) the fact that if George is either not a man or is not a bassoon player or both, the conjunction is false. However, this conjunction is about George solely in virtue of the *second* conjunct's being about George. And since it is the first conjunct that is the existence statement, that the *conjunction* is about George does not show that the *existence statement* "There exist men who play the bassoon" is about George even if the speaker does intend to make a statement which is about George when he makes this statement. That the speaker is not referring to a particular individual in making the existence statement "There exist men who play the bassoon" is shown by the fact that the hearer could appropriately ask "Which men play the bassoon?" but not "Which men do you mean?". Moreover, even the speaker's believing that George is the *only* man who plays the bassoon does not render this statement one which is about George. For this statement can still be true even if this belief is false. If this statement were about George in the required way, this statement could not be true if George were not a bassoon player.

It might now be objected that the existence statement can still be about a particular individual at least in a certain sort of situation, namely that in which there is one and only one individual having the properties mentioned in the existence statement. For example, if the speaker says "There are men who are six feet tall" and there is one and only one man who is six feet tall, then this statement is about that man. But why should it be said that this statement is about this individual? The argument for this is (*a*) it is the existence of this particular individual that renders this statement true and (*b*) there is a close relation between what it is that renders a statement true and what it is that that statement is about.

The objector's position—that there are situations in which an existence statement can be or is about a particular individual—is one which I think that we must take very seriously. For it is founded on a principle which I think is correct, namely the principle that there is a close connection between aboutness and truth-value dependence. The theory of aboutness which I will present in the next section is based on just this principle. In discussing the objector's position, I will give an argument intended to show that even in such situations existence statements are not about particular individuals, at least in the way in which subject–predicate statements are about particular individuals.

As explained in earlier chapters, I have been using the term 'statement' in such a way that which individual a statement is about serves as a criterion of individuation for statements. Two statements may be two different statements just because they are about different individuals. In order to be making the same statement, two speakers must be saying something about the same individual. Now let us take a situation in which individual H is the only individual in the world. Statement S can be about H in this situation. And S can and will be about H when there are many other individuals besides H in the world too. Now let us compare this with existence statement E, namely "There is an individual who is $\emptyset$ and Θ". According to the view being examined, if there is only one individual G who has $\emptyset$ and Θ, E is about that individual. But if there are many such individuals, E is not about any of them. Yet E is the same statement, regardless of how many individuals there are having these properties. In this respect, S and E are very different from one another. S has to be about the individual it is about simply in order to be S. But E can be about a particular individual or not be about a particular individual and still be E. Being about H is essential for S but being about G is not essential for E. I think that this constitutes good grounds for claiming that E is not about individuals in the way that S is. And I think that we may say this even while admitting that the truth-value of E might depend on G's properties in some cases.[1] Being about H is fundamental to S but being about G is not fundamental to E. So if we still want to say that E is about G in some situations (such as those described in the footnote to the sentence preceding this one), it seems reasonable to say that E is still not about G in the way in which S is about H. E is not about G in a way which makes E the statement that it is.

[1] There are two sorts of cases in which E's truth-value might be said to depend on G's properties: (1) G is the only individual having $\emptyset$ and Θ, in which case the proponent of this view would say that G's properties make E true; (2) G is the only individual that exists and G lacks $\emptyset$ or Θ or both, in which case G's properties would be said to make E false.

Thus, a theory of aboutness, where the aboutness in question is the sort essential to subject–predicate statements, must show that existence statements do not have this sort of aboutness. But this is not all that such a theory should show. We must also explain why it seems plausible to say that E is about G in some situations, particularly when G is the only individual to have $\emptyset$ and Θ.

3 *The nature of aboutness*

Now I want to suggest a theory of aboutness based on the principle that there is a close relation between aboutness and truth-value dependence. Consider the case of the existence statement "There are men who are Columbia graduates". Let us suppose that this statement is false. When this statement is false, no individual has the properties of being a man and being a Columbia graduate. And yet this existence statement has a truth-value in this case since it is false in this case. So this statement is not false in virtue of the properties of any individual. It is true that if there is one and only one individual who is a man and is a Columbia graduate, then the existence statement is true and its truth perhaps can in such a case be said to depend on the properties of a particular individual. For it can, with plausibility, be said that this statement is true *because* that individual has the properties mentioned in the statement. But it cannot be said that when this statement is false, it is false because a certain particular individual lacks the properties mentioned in the statement. For which of the many individuals who lack these properties shall we pick out as being *the* individual in virtue of whose lack of these properties this statement is false? There is no way of doing this in a world which contains more than one individual. So the following theory of aboutness would seem to be a good beginning towards a theory which will distinguish between existence statements and subject–predicate statements with respect to aboutness: A statement is about an individual if and only if (*a*) if that statement is true, it is true in virtue of that individual's having the properties mentioned in the statement, or (*b*) if that statement is false, it is false in virtue of that individual's lacking those properties. By 'properties mentioned in the statement' in (*a*), I mean the following: (i) for subject–predicate statements, these properties are the properties mentioned in the predicate of the statement; for it is in virtue of the individual's having these that the statement is true; (ii) for existence statements, these properties are all of the properties mentioned after 'There exists'; for an individual must have every such property in order for the statement to be true.

Does this theory of aboutness show what such a theory ought to show? Such a theory ought to show that existence statements are *never in any circumstances* about single individuals. But the above theory does not reply at all to the objector's position. The above theory leaves it open for existence statements to be about individuals *sometimes*, just as the objector claims they are. For example, in a case in which there is just one man who is a Columbia graduate, the statement "There exists a man who is a Columbia graduate" fulfils condition (*a*). This statement is true because that individual has those properties. So in this situation this statement is about an individual even if this statement is not about particular individuals in other situations (namely, when more than one individual has these properties). Even when this existence statement is false, it can be about an individual, according to the above theory. Consider a world which contains one and only one individual and this individual is neither a man nor a Columbia graduate. This existence statement is false in such a world because this individual does not have those properties. Thus, condition (*b*) is fulfilled. So in this case, too, this existence statement is about an individual, even though this statement would be about no individual in a world containing more than one individual none of which has these properties.

I think that this shows that if we are to capture the kind of aboutness that subject–predicate statements have, we must modify the above simple theory. I will do so in the following way: I will say "A statement is about an individual in a particular situation S if and only if (1) (*a*) if that statement is true in S, it is true in S in virtue of that individual's having the properties mentioned in the statement, or (*b*) if that statement is false in S, it is false in S because that individual lacks those properties; and (11) every possible situation in which that statement has a truth-value is a situation in which the statement has the truth-value which it has because a particular individual has or lacks certain properties". Roughly speaking, this new formulation is intended to ensure that a statement is not about an individual in situation S unless it is about an individual in every possible situation in which it has a truth-value. This condition is met by subject–predicate statements but not by existence statements. As we have seen, the truth-value of existence statements can be said to depend in some situations on the properties of a particular, specifiable individual but not in all situations. For example, in a case in which more than one individual has the properties mentioned in the existence statement, the statement is not true in virtue of one of these individuals having those properties. But the truth-value of a subject–predicate statement always, in every possible situation, depends on some individual's having the properties mentioned in the statement.

Two remarks must be made about the relation between this theory of aboutness and subject–predicate statements. First, this theory allows the possibility of a subject–predicate statement having no truth-value in certain possible worlds. This is the import of the phrase in condition (11) 'every possible situation *in which that statement has a truth-value*'. The theory allows a statement to be about an individual in S even if it is not about an individual in every possible world. Second, this theory allows necessary statements to be about individuals. In Chapter V, I said that on my use of the term 'statement', a necessary statement is a statement attributing a property to an individual which that individual necessarily has. Such statements cannot be false. But they are still true because the individual in question has the property in question. And so they are about such individuals.

Finally, it must be noted that our theory gives an explanation of two things. First, it explains why, in a situation in which only one man is a Columbia graduate, the statement "There is a man who is a Columbia graduate" seems to be about that man—or, better, why the claim that this existence statement is about this individual in this situation has some plausibility. On our theory, aboutness is closely related to truth-value dependence. And in the situation just described, the truth-value of this existence statement may seem to depend on that individual's properties. This may not only seem to be but also in fact be a *kind* of aboutness, the kind that existence statements have in such situations. But, secondly, there is another sort of aboutness—the sort that subject–predicate statements have. And our theory shows what this type of aboutness consists in and how it differs from the sort that existence statements may sometimes have. The relation between these two kinds of aboutness is in fact just the relation between the two formulations of the theory of aboutness presented in this section.

CONCLUSION

Now I want to summarize very briefly what I have tried to do in this book. After pointing to the problem of ambiguous reference and arguing against the claim that there is no such thing as reference, I criticized the Context Theory as being completely inadequate. The Abbreviation Theory was then elaborated and defended at some length. But in the course of setting forth this theory, it became clear that it is not sufficient merely to say that names (or descriptions) are abbreviations of descriptions. For one name can abbreviate descriptions which uniquely fit two different individuals. Hence something more is needed to explain why the use of that name results in a reference to one of these individuals rather than to the other. At this point I introduced the notion of using a name *in a certain meaning*. But what is it to use a name in a certain meaning? I believe that the speaker's intentions must be brought in to explain this. But having introduced the speaker's intentions at this point, I went on to develop a theory of referring which mentions only the speaker's intentions and has no need to regard names and descriptions as abbreviations.

One main point, then, of what I have said is that in many cases the connection between uses of language and the world comes about through the speaker's intentions. This is not a phenomenon which is confined to referring either. The speaker's intentions enter into other types of linguistic situations as well. For example, when a speaker uses an ambiguous word (such as 'bear') or an ambiguous sentence where there is no question of ambiguity of reference, what he is saying is often decided by what he intended to say. But this point about intentions must not be over-emphasized. Ultimately, successful reference in ambiguous situations also depends on something beyond (though closely related to) the speaker's intentions. For successful reference in ambiguous cases requires that the speaker's intention itself not be ambiguous. The speaker's intention must be, so to speak, "aimed at" one particular individual. And this cannot ultimately depend on yet further intentions. At some point there must be an intention which "aims itself" at a particular individual. And this occurs when the thought of the individual associated with that intention fits one and only one individual. If this thought of the individual is regarded as being essentially related to a description—what I have called "the intention description"—and if a description is regarded as an essentially linguistic entity, then in this way language (or this type of linguistic expression, the description) is what relates a particular use of language to a particular individual. But it must not be forgotten that the description cannot do this by itself. It does this because it is an *intention* description—because it is closely related to the speaker's intentions. Thus, intentions have a major role in relating uses of language to the world.

INDEX

International Library of Philosophy & Scientific Method

Editor: Ted Honderich

List of titles, page two

International Library of Psychology Philosophy & Scientific Method

Editor: C K Ogden

List of titles, page six

ROUTLEDGE AND KEGAN PAUL LTD
68 Carter Lane London EC4

International Library of Philosophy and Scientific Method
(*Demy 8vo*)

Allen, R. E. (Ed.)
Studies in Plato's Metaphysics
Contributors: J. L. Ackrill, R. E. Allen, R. S. Bluck, H. F. Cherniss, F. M. Cornford, R. C. Cross, P. T. Geach, R. Hackforth, W. F. Hicken, A. C. Lloyd, G. R. Morrow, G. E. L. Owen, G. Ryle, W. G. Runciman, G. Vlastos
464 pp. 1965. (2nd Impression 1967.) 70s.

Armstrong, D. M.
Perception and the Physical World
208 pp. 1961. (3rd Impression 1966.) 25s.
A Materialist Theory of the Mind
376 pp. 1967. (2nd Impression 1969.) 50s.

Bambrough, Renford (Ed.)
New Essays on Plato and Aristotle
Contributors: J. L. Ackrill, G. E. M. Anscombe, Renford Bambrough, R. M. Hare, D. M. MacKinnon, G. E. L. Owen, G. Ryle, G. Vlastos
184 pp. 1965. (2nd Impression 1967.) 28s.

Barry, Brian
Political Argument
382 pp. 1965. (3rd Impression 1968.) 50s.

Bird, Graham
Kant's Theory of Knowledge:
An Outline of One Central Argument in the *Critique of Pure Reason*
220 pp. 1962. (2nd Impression 1965.) 28s.

Brentano, Franz
The True and the Evident
Edited and narrated by Professor R. Chisholm
218 pp. 1965. 40s.

The Origin of Our Knowledge of Right and Wrong
Edited by Oskar Kraus. English edition edited by Roderick M. Chisholm. Translated by Roderick M. Chisholm and Elizabeth H. Schneewind
174 pp. 1969. 40s.

Broad, C. D.
Lectures on Physical Research
Incorporating the Perrott Lectures given in Cambridge University in 1959 and 1960
461 pp. 1962. (2nd Impression 1966.) 56s.

Crombie, I. M.
An Examination of Plato's Doctrine
1. Plato on Man and Society
408 pp. 1962. (3rd Impression 1969.) 42s.
II. Plato on Knowledge and Reality
583 pp. 1963. (2nd Impression 1967.) 63s.

International Library of Philosophy and Scientific Method
(*Demy 8vo*)

Day, John Patrick
Inductive Probability
352 pp. 1961. 40s.

Dretske, Fred I.
Seeing and Knowing
270 pp. 1969. 35s.

Ducasse, C. J.
Truth, Knowledge and Causation
263 pp. 1969. 50s.

Edel, Abraham
Method in Ethical Theory
379 pp. 1963. 32s.

Fann, K. T. (Ed.)
Symposium on J. L. Austin
Contributors: A. J. Ayer, Jonathan Bennett, Max Black, Stanley Cavell,
Walter Cerf, Roderick M. Chisholm, L. Jonathan Cohen, Roderick Firth, L. W.
Forguson, Mats Furberg, Stuart Hampshire, R. J. Hirst, C. G. New, P. H.
Nowell-Smith, David Pears, John Searle, Peter Strawson, Irving Thalberg,
J. O. Urmson, G. J. Warnock, Jon Wheatly, Alan White
512 pp. 1969.

Flew, Anthony
Hume's Philosophy of Belief
A Study of his First "Inquiry"
269 pp. 1961. (2nd Impression 1966.) 30s.

Fogelin, Robert J.
Evidence and Meaning
Studies in Analytical Philosophy
200 pp. 1967. 25s.

Gale, Richard
The Language of Time
256 pp. 1968. 40s.

Goldman, Lucien
The Hidden God
A Study of Tragic Vision in the *Pensées* of Pascal and the Tragedies of Racine.
Translated from the French by Philip Thody
424 pp. 1964. 70s.

Hamlyn, D. W.
Sensation and Perception
A History of the Philosophy of Perception
222 pp. 1961. (3rd Impression 1967.) 25s.

2*

International Library of Philosophy and Scientific Method
(*Demy 8vo*)

Kemp, J.
Reason, Action and Morality
216 pp. 1964. 30s.

Körner, Stephan
Experience and Theory
An Essay in the Philosophy of Science
272 pp. 1966. (2nd Impression 1969.) 45s.

Lazerowitz, Morris
Studies in Metaphilosophy
276 pp. 1964. 35s.

Linsky, Leonard
Referring
152 pp. 1968. 35s.

MacIntosh, J. J., and Coval, S. C. (Ed.)
The Business of Reason
280 pp. 1969. 42s.

Merleau-Ponty, M.
Phenomenology of Perception
Translated from the French by Colin Smith
487 pp. 1962. (4th Impression 1967.) 56s.

Perelman, Chaim
The Idea of Justice and the Problem of Argument
Introduction by H. L. A. Hart. Translated from the French by John Petrie
224 pp. 1963. 28s.

Ross, Alf
Directives, Norms and their Logic
192 pp. 1967. 35s.

Schlesinger, G.
Method in the Physical Sciences
148 pp. 1963. 21s.

Sellars, W. F.
Science, Perception and Reality
374 pp. 1963. (2nd Impression 1966.) 50s.

Shwayder, D. S.
The Stratification of Behaviour
A System of Definitions Propounded and Defended
428 pp. 1965. 56s.

Skolimowski, Henryk
Polish Analytical Philosophy
288 pp. 1967. 40s.

4

International Library of Philosophy and Scientific Method
(*Demy 8vo*)

Smart, J. J. C.
Philosophy and Scientific Realism
168 pp. 1963. (3rd Impression 1967.) 25s.

Smythies, J. R. (Ed.)
Brain and Mind
Contributors: Lord Brain, John Beloff, C. J. Ducasse, Antony Flew, Hartwig
Kuhlenbeck, D. M. MacKay, H. H. Price, Anthony Quinton and J. R. Smythies
288 pp. 1965. 40s.

Science and E.S.P.
Contributors: Gilbert Murray, H. H. Price, Rosalind Heywood, Cyril Burt,
C. D. Broad, Francis Huxley and John Beloff
320 pp. about 40s.

Taylor, Charles
The Explanation of Behaviour
288 pp. 1964. (2nd Impression 1965.) 40s.

Williams, Bernard, and Montefiore, Alan
British Analytical Philosophy
352 pp. 1965. (2nd Impression 1967.) 45s.

Winch, Peter (Ed.)
Studies in the Philosophy of Wittgenstein
Contributors: Hidé Ishiguro, Rush Rhees, D. S. Shwayder, John W. Cook,
L. R. Reinhardt and Anthony Manser
224 pp. 1969.

Wittgenstein, Ludwig
Tractatus Logico-Philosophicus
The German text of the *Logisch-Philosophische Abhandlung* with a new
translation by D. F. Pears and B. F. McGuinness. Introduction by
Bertrand Russell
188 pp. 1961. (3rd Impression 1966.) 21s.

Wright, Georg Henrik Von
Norm and Action
A Logical Enquiry. The Gifford Lectures
232 pp. 1963. (2nd Impression 1964.) 32s.

The Varieties of Goodness
The Gifford Lectures
236 pp. 1963. (3rd Impression 1966.) 28s.

Zinkernagel, Peter
Conditions for Description
Translated from the Danish by Olaf Lindum
272 pp. 1962. 37s. 6d.

International Library of Psychology, Philosophy, and Scientific Method
(*Demy 8vo*)

PHILOSOPHY

Anton, John Peter
Aristotle's Theory of Contrariety
276 pp. 1957. 25s.

Black, Max
The Nature of Mathematics
A Critical Survey
242 pp. 1933. (5th Impression 1965.) 28s.

Bluck, R. S.
Plato's Phaedo
A Translation with Introduction, Notes and Appendices
226 pp. 1955. 21s.

Broad, C. D.
Five Types of Ethical Theory
322 pp. 1930. (9th Impression 1967.) 30s.

The Mind and Its Place in Nature
694 pp. 1925. (7th Impression 1962.) 70s. See also Lean, Martin

Buchler, Justus (Ed.)
The Philosophy of Peirce
Selected Writings
412 pp. 1940. (3rd Impression 1956.) 35s.

Burtt, E. A.
The Metaphysical Foundations of Modern Physical Science
A Historical and Critical Essay
364 pp. 2nd (revised) edition 1932. (5th Impression 1964.) 35s.

Carnap, Rudolf
The Logical Syntax of Language
Translated from the German by Amethe Smeaton
376 pp. 1937. (7th Impression 1967.) 40s.

Chwistek, Leon
The Limits of Science
Outline of Logic and of the Methodology of the Exact Sciences
With Introduction and Appendix by Helen Charlotte Brodie
414 pp. 2nd edition 1949. 32s.

Cornford, F. M.
Plato's Theory of Knowledge
The Theaetetus and Sophist of Plato
Translated with a running commentary
358 pp. 1935. (7th Impression 1967.) 28s.

6

International Library of Psychology, Philosophy, and Scientific Method
(*Demy 8vo*)

Cornford, F. M. (*continued*)
Plato's Cosmology
The Timaeus of Plato
Translated with a running commentary
402 pp. Frontispiece. 1937. (5th Impression 1966.) 45s.

Plato and Parmenides
Parmenides' *Way of Truth* and Plato's *Parmenides*
Translated with a running commentary
280 pp. 1939. (5th Impression 1964.) 32s.

Crawshay-Williams, Rupert
Methods and Criteria of Reasoning
An Inquiry into the Structure of Controversy
312 pp. 1957. 32s.

Fritz, Charles A.
Bertrand Russell's Construction of the External World
252 pp. 1952. 30s.

Hulme, T. E.
Speculations
Essays on Humanism and the Philosophy of Art
Edited by Herbert Read. Foreword and Frontispiece by Jacob Epstein
296 pp. 2nd edition 1936. (6th Impression 1965.) 40s.

Lazerowitz, Morris
The Structure of Metaphysics
With a Foreword by John Wisdom
262 pp. 1955. (2nd Impression 1963.) 30s.

Lodge, Rupert C.
Plato's Theory of Art
332 pp. 1953. 25s.

Mannheim, Karl
Ideology and Utopia
An Introduction to the Sociology of Knowledge
With a Preface by Louis Wirth. Translated from the German by Louis Wirth
and Edward Shils
360 pp. 1954. (2nd Impression 1966.) 30s.

Moore, G. E.
Philosophical Studies
360 pp. 1922. (6th Impression 1965.) 35s. See also Ramsey, F. P.

International Library of Psychology, Philosophy, and Scientific Method
(*Demy 8vo*)

Ogden, C. K., and Richards, I. A.
The Meaning of Meaning
A Study of the Influence of Language upon Thought and of the Science of Symbolism
With supplementary essays by B. Malinowski and F. G. Crookshank
394 pp. 10th Edition 1949. (6th Impression 1967.) 32s.
See also Bentham, J.

Peirce, Charles, *see* Buchler, J.

Ramsey, Frank Plumpton
The Foundations of Mathematics and other Logical Essays
Edited by R. B. Braithwaite. Preface by G. E. Moore
318 pp. 1931. (4th Impression 1965.) 35s.

Richards, I. A.
Principles of Literary Criticism
312 pp. 2nd Edition. 1926. (17th Impression 1966.) 30s.

Mencius on the Mind. Experiments in Multiple Definition
190 pp. 1932. (2nd Impression 1964.) 28s.

Russell, Bertrand, *see* Fritz, C. A.; Lange, F. A.; Wittgenstein, L.

Smart, Ninian
Reasons and Faiths
An Investigation of Religious Discourse, Christian and Non-Christian
230 pp. 1958. (2nd Impression 1965.) 28s.

Vaihinger, H.
The Philosophy of As If
A System of the Theoretical, Practical and Religious Fictions of Mankind
Translated by C. K. Ogden
428 pp. 2nd edition 1935. (4th Impression 1965.) 45s.

Wittgenstein, Ludwig
Tractatus Logico-Philosophicus
With an Introduction by Bertrand Russell, F.R.S., German text with an English translation en regard
216 pp. 1922. (9th Impression 1962.) 21s.
For the Pears-McGuinness translation—*see page 5*

Wright, Georg Henrik von
Logical Studies
214 pp. 1957. (2nd Impression 1967.) 28s.

International Library of Psychology, Philosophy, and Scientific Method
(*Demy 8vo*)

Zeller, Eduard
Outlines of the History of Greek Philosophy
Revised by Dr. Wilhelm Nestle. Translated from the German by L. R. Palmer
248 pp. 13th (revised) edition 1931. (5th Impression 1963.) 28s.

PSYCHOLOGY

Adler, Alfred
The Practice and Theory of Individual Psychology
Translated by P. Radin
368 pp. 2nd (revised) edition 1929. (8th Impression 1964.) 30s.

Eng, Helga
The Psychology of Children's Drawings
From the First Stroke to the Coloured Drawing
240 pp. 8 colour plates. 139 figures. 2nd edition 1954. (3rd Impression 1966.) 40s.

Koffka, Kurt
The Growth of the Mind
An Introduction to Child-Psychology
Translated from the German by Robert Morris Ogden
456 pp 16 figures. 2nd edition (revised) 1928. (6th Impression 1965.) 45s.

Principles of Gestalt Psychology
740 pp. 112 figures. 39 tables. 1935. (5th Impression 1962.) 60s.

Malinowski, Bronislaw
Crime and Custom in Savage Society
152 pp. 6 plates. 1926. (8th Impression 1966.) 21s.

Sex and Repression in Savage Society
290 pp. 1927. (4th Impression 1953.) 30s.
See also Ogden, C. K.

Murphy, Gardner
An Historical Introduction to Modern Psychology
488 pp. 5th edition (revised) 1949. (6th Impression 1967.) 40s.

Paget, R.
Human Speech
Some Observations, Experiments, and Conclusions as to the Nature, Origin, Purpose and Possible Improvement of Human Speech
374 pp. 5 plates. 1930. (2nd Impression 1963.) 42s.

Petermann, Bruno
The Gestalt Theory and the Problem of Configuration
Translated from the German by Meyer Fortes
364 pp. 20 figures. 1932. (2nd Impression 1950.) 25s.

Piaget, Jean
The Language and Thought of the Child
Preface by E. Claparède. Translated from the French by Marjorie Gabain
220 pp. 3rd edition (revised and enlarged) 1959. (3rd Impression 1966.) 30s.

Judgment and Reasoning in the Child
Translated from the French by Marjorie Warden
276 pp. 1928. (5th Impression 1969.) 30s.

The Child's Conception of the World
Translated from the French by Joan and Andrew Tomlinson
408 pp. 1929. (4th Impression 1964.) 40s.

The Child's Conception of Physical Causality
Translated from the French by Marjorie Gabain
(3rd Impression 1965.) 30s.

The Moral Judgment of the Child
Translated from the French by Marjorie Gabain
438 pp. 1932. (4th Impression 1965.) 35s.

The Psychology of Intelligence
Translated from the French by Malcolm Piercy and D. E. Berlyne
198 pp. 1950. (4th Impression 1964.) 18s.

The Child's Conception of Number
Translated from the French by C. Gattegno and F. M. Hodgson
266 pp. 1952. (3rd Impression 1964.) 25s.

The Origin of Intelligence in the Child
Translated from the French by Margaret Cook
448 pp. 1953. (2nd Impression 1966.) 42s.

The Child's Conception of Geometry
In collaboration with Bärbel Inhelder and Alina Szeminska. Translated from the French by E. A. Lunzer
428 pp. 1960. (2nd Impression 1966.) 45s.

Piaget, Jean, and Inhelder, Bärbel
The Child's Conception of Space
Translated from the French by F. J. Langdon and J. L. Lunzer
512 pp. 29 figures. 1956. (3rd Impression 1967.) 42s.

Roback, A. A.
The Psychology of Character
With a Survey of Personality in General
786 pp. 3rd edition (revised and enlarged 1952.) 50s.

Smythies, J. R.
Analysis of Perception
With a Preface by Sir Russell Brain, Bt.
162 pp. 1956. 21s.

International Library of Psychology, Philosophy, and Scientific Method
(*Demy 8vo*)

van der Hoop, J. H.
Character and the Unconscious
A Critical Exposition of the Psychology of Freud and Jung
Translated from the German by Elizabeth Trevelyan
240 pp. 1923. (2nd Impression 1950.) 20s.

Woodger, J. H.
Biological Principles
508 pp. 1929. (Re-issued with a new Introduction 1966.) 60s.

PRINTED BY HEADLEY BROTHERS LTD 109 KINGSWAY LONDON WC2 AND ASHFORD KENT